star power

Always Dreamin'

Catch Star's act!

★ **Supernova**

★ **Always Dreamin'**

Coming Soon

★ **Never Give Up**

All Simon and Schuster Books are available by post from:
Simon & Schuster Cash Sales. PO Box 29
Douglas, Isle of Man IM99 1BQ
Credit cards accepted.
Please telephone 01624 677237
fax 01624 670923, Internet
http://www.bookpost.co.uk or email:
bookshop@enterprise.net for details

star power

Catherine
Hapka

Always Dreamin'

SIMON AND SCHUSTER

SIMON AND SCHUSTER

First published in Great Britain by Simon & Schuster UK Ltd, 2004
A Viacom company

Originally published in the USA in 2004 by Aladdin Paperbacks,
an imprint of Simon & Schuster Children's Division, New York.
Copyright © by Catherine Hapka, 2004

1 3 5 7 9 10 8 6 4 2

Simon & Schuster UK Ltd
Africa House
64-78 Kingsway
London WC2B 6AH

A CIP catalogue record for this book is available
from the British Library

ISBN 0 689 87297 6

Printed and bound in Great Britain by Bookmarque, Croydon, Surrey.

star power

Always Dreamin'

One

Star Calloway yawned and glanced up from her book. The clock on the wall of her temporary dressing room said it was just after 8:00 p.m.

I wonder if I have time to call Nans or Missy before I go onstage? she wondered sleepily. *Let's see – if it's eight p.m. here in London, that means that back in Pennsylvania it's . . . um . . .*

She knew she should know the answer – she'd been in London, England, for nearly a week – but she didn't have the strength to do the maths just then. Fourteen-year-old Star had been a singing superstar for almost a year and was used to long days and late nights. But headlining her first world tour was turning out to be more tiring than she'd expected. Even in the first week she'd already had to adjust to major time changes and lots of boring travelling, and still had to find the energy to sing and dance her heart out onstage every other night or so.

Despite the exhausting schedule, though, Star was having a wonderful time. She loved performing for a live audience more than almost anything else in the world, and the crowds at her three sold-out concerts in London had been bigger and more enthusiastic than any audience she'd had so far. She couldn't wait to get to the next stop on the tour, which was Edinburgh, Scotland.

But before her entourage left London the next day, Star had one more performance – this one on the *Youth of Britain* awards show. The Yobbies, as they were commonly called, were presented to young musicians from all over Great Britain. As an American, Star wasn't eligible to win any Yobbies herself, but she'd been invited to sing one of her current hits as part of the show, which was being televised live from a fancy new concert hall at the exclusive Londonia Hotel.

Star glanced around her dressing room. A large make-up counter dominated one wall, its light-rimmed mirror reflecting every detail of the small, windowless room. Upon their arrival an hour earlier, Star's stylist, Lola LaRue, had dumped most of the contents of her make-up bag onto the counter, along with various hair dryers and other implements.

Meanwhile Star herself was sitting at one end of a comfortable plush sofa. Her dog, a plump fawn pug named Dudley Do-Wrong, was lying on the floor at her feet gnawing happily on his favourite white plastic bone, which he had been carrying everywhere since the start of the tour. The sofa faced a boxy TV that looked as if it dated from sometime just after World War II. At the moment the TV's flickering screen showed the action on the main stage of the concert hall upstairs. Behind the TV stood a brass-coloured clothing rack holding jackets, spare bits of Star's stage costume, a couple of tuxedos, and some other clothes. Several other chairs, tables, and sofas were scattered around the room, and at one end of the make-up counter a frosted glass door led into a small bathroom.

Near the door leading out into the hall, which was closed at the moment, Star's manager, Mike Mosley, was sitting at a small table playing cards with her driver and head bodyguard, Tank Massimo. Mike had a bushy mustache and intelligent green eyes, and he was wearing purple cowboy boots that added at least an inch to his already impressive height. Next to Mike, Tank looked about half as tall – but made up for it by also being twice as broad. His muscles rippled beneath his fitted shirt as he shuffled the cards he was holding.

"No sixes," he said smugly. "Go fish."

Mike grumbled under his breath and glanced over at Star. "Sure you don't want us to deal you in, sweetheart?" he asked. "Might be a while before you go on."

"Thanks, Mike," Star said. "I'll pass. I'm supposed to be reading up on the history of Hadrian's Wall. Mrs Nattle warned me she's going to quiz me on it during the ride up to Scotland tomorrow."

Soon after the release of her first album, *Star Power,* Star had realized that she would probably never be able to go back to school like a normal kid her age. Instead she had a full-time tutor. Mike, Tank, and the other adults on Star's team called Mrs Magdalene Nattle by her nickname, Mags, but Star always referred to her as Mrs Nattle.

Star stifled another yawn and glanced at the TV screen, wondering how long it would be before it was her turn to perform. Onscreen she saw a pretty girl about her own age step onto the stage and walk to the podium. The girl was dressed in a flashy silvery gown, her thick dark hair piled into an elaborate do on top of her head. Vibrant red lipstick and smoky eye shadow emphasized her pouty expression. She was carrying a large white envelope.

"Hey, check it," Star called to Mike and Tank. "Jade is here."

Mike nodded. "Heard she might be," he said, shuffling his cards carefully. "She's not performing, though – just presenting."

"Cool," Star said. "Maybe I'll finally get to meet her."

She watched the other girl curiously. Jade had released her first album just a few months earlier and was one of the hottest new acts in the United States. Her album was currently number three on the charts, right behind Star's second album, *Supernova,* and the latest album by longtime teen superstar Eddie Urbane. Ever since she'd seen Jade's first video, Star had hoped to meet her. She was sure they would have a lot in common. Star's best friend, Missy Takamori, had even joked that Jade would make a perfect new best friend for Star. While Star had absolutely no intention of replacing Missy, she had to admit that it would be nice to hang out once in a while with someone her age who really understood what her day-to-day life was like.

Soon Jade finished her duties and left the stage, and Star

tried once again to focus on the book on her lap. As she scanned the page looking for where she'd left off, Dudley suddenly looked up alertly. The little dog let out a short yip, and a second later there was a brisk knock on the dressing room door.

"Yikes!" Star dropped her book back onto her lap. "I hope they're not coming to tell me I'm on. Lola still hasn't finished my hair!"

She glanced over at her reflection in the make-up mirror. Her own familiar pretty, blue-eyed face looked back at her. Instead of its usual cloud of curly, silvery-blonde hair, though, it was framed by a mass of hot rollers. Lola had set her hair before hurrying off in search of more styling gel. Star could never quite understand why she needed hot rollers and styling gel when her hair was naturally curly, but she trusted Lola to know best about anything having to do with hair, make-up, or clothes.

"Don't fret," Mike said in his calm Texas drawl. He patted his shirt pocket, which held one of the several cell phones he always carried. "Lola just called from upstairs and said they're running late, remember? Like I said, you won't be going on for quite a spell."

Dudley let out a few more barks and wagged his stubby, curly tail as Tank opened the door. A pleasant-looking young woman was standing outside. She had a yellow badge reading STAFF on her lapel and was holding a large fruit basket topped with an elaborate stars-and-stripes bow.

"Evening, all," the woman chirped cheerfully in a crisp British accent. She spotted Star and took a step towards her, her smile widening. "Welcome to the Yobbies, Miss Calloway. The management wanted to send you a few things to make you more comfortable while you wait, and to show you our appreciation for coming tonight."

"Thank you," Star said politely, expecting the woman to set down the large fruit basket and leave.

Instead the woman turned and gestured to someone behind her. "Bring it in, mates," she called.

Star blinked as three men entered, each of them carrying a matching but even larger basket. Dudley danced around at their feet, his long pink tongue lolling eagerly as he did his best to trip them all.

"Wow," Star said as she noticed a portable CD player poking out of one of the baskets. She still wasn't entirely used to receiving expensive gifts from strangers, even though

Mike had assured her many times that it was just one of the side benefits of being a celebrity. "Thanks again," she told the woman.

The men hurried out of the room. "Ta. Enjoy," the woman told Star with a smile before backing out herself and closing the door behind her.

Mike glanced up from his cards. "Get anything good?"

Star tossed her book on a table and stood up. Digging through the closest basket, she found a pink leather jacket, half a dozen CDs, and a gold bracelet with tiny charms representing famous British sights.

"Check this out," she said, admiring the charm bracelet's miniature copy of the Tower of London. She had toured the real thing the afternoon before with Mags, learning all about its role in the sometimes bloody history of old London. She stepped over Dudley, who had gone back to chewing on his bone, to show the men.

"Bling bling," Tank commented with a chuckle. "Looks like some good stuff, Star-baby."

She dug into the next basket. This one contained mostly food – unfamiliar British sodas in colourful glass bottles, fancy candies of every variety imaginable, and even a small jar containing glossy black beads of real caviar.

"Oh," she said with a gasp as she uncovered a package of chocolate-covered peanuts. "Mom always loved these . . ."

Her free hand wandered to the silver star necklace that she always wore. The necklace had been the last gift she'd ever got from her parents before their mysterious disappearance two years earlier. Mr and Mrs Calloway, along with Star's baby brother, Timmy, had been on vacation in Florida when their small rented boat had disappeared during a sudden storm. Star had been in New York with Mike at the time, auditioning for Flashpoint Records. She had landed the contract, but she lost her parents on the very same day. Despite the fact that the police in Florida still had no idea what had happened to the Calloways, Star had never given up on finding them again someday. She knew they were still out there; she wore her optimism as constantly as she wore that star necklace, never giving up hope even for a second. That way, it was as if her family were always with her in spirit.

Still, she would have traded all her fame and fortune to have them with her in person as well . . .

Mike was watching her closely. "Chin up," he said, his gruff voice gentler than usual. "Remember, *we* know how much you miss them – even if nobody else does."

Star's eyes suddenly filled with tears. She leaned down and hugged Dudley so hard that the little dog dropped his bone and let out a strangled squeak. Being a pop superstar wasn't always easy. In addition to the long hours, she had to deal with constant attention from the press, the occasional bad review or unflattering article, and an almost complete lack of privacy. But for Star the hardest part of all was keeping her true family history a secret. Aside from the police in Florida, her friends and her grandmother back in New Limpet, Pennsylvania, and a handful of private detectives she had hired, almost no one knew about the Calloways' disappearance. Mike had seen to that.

"It's weird," she said with a sigh, letting go of Dudley and touching her necklace again. "I always miss Mom and Dad and Timmy. But it's worse, somehow, being on the road like this."

"That's only natural," Mike said sympathetically, setting down his cards. "You're seein' new things, new places. Makes sense that you'd wish they were here with you."

Tank nodded. "Remember, Star-baby, you can always talk to Mike or me about it whenever you're feeling down. Or Mags."

"I know," Star said. "And don't worry, I'm not going to blab about it to anyb—"

She cut herself off as the dressing room door flew open and a wildly dressed African-American woman burst in. The woman was wearing a denim jacket with a vintage lace skirt and black combat boots. Countless bracelets jingled on her pleasantly plump arms, and half a dozen earrings dangled from each ear. Her hair was streaked with purple highlights that matched her dramatic eyeshadow.

"Don't panic, anyone – I'm back!" Lola LaRue exclaimed breathlessly, waving her hands. Each of her long fake finger-nails was decorated with a tiny Union Jack in honour of Star's visit to England.

Lola had only joined Star's entourage a few months earlier, and even though she'd already become an integral part of the team, she still didn't know about Star's unusual family background. Nobody had a bad word to say about Lola's talents with clothes, hair, and make-up – under her care, Star always looked fresh and flawless. But the always enthusiastic Lola had a bad habit of blurting out breathless – and only occasionally accurate – pronouncements to the press at any given moment. Because of that, Mike still didn't trust her with Star's full history. Star always felt bad keeping the truth from Lola, who already felt like family herself. But she trusted that Mike knew best, so she obeyed his wishes.

"They're trying to catch up, so they want us to be ready in half an hour," Lola told Mike. She rolled her eyes, letting out an inelegant snort. "But if they're really ready for Star by then, I'll eat your cowboy boots."

Mike chuckled. "Might as well make sure she's ready, though," he pointed out. "Don't want her to have to rush onstage with rollers in her hair."

"Hey, why not?" Lola joked in return. "Our girl here could get away with it if anyone could. She might even start a trend!" She winked at Star and patted the bench in front of the make-up mirror. "Come on, babydoll – let's get you looking like a pop princess so Mike can stop his fretting."

Star stood up and walked over to Lola, grabbing her handheld computer from an end table as she passed. While Lola fussed with her hair, Star logged on to the little machine and quickly typed out an e-mail:

From: singingstar01

To: MissTaka

Subject: Are u there?

Just checking in. Write back when u can.

xxoo

Star

She pressed SEND. After a moment the machine emitted a shrill error beep. MESSAGE UNDELIVERABLE flashed on the tiny screen.

Star sighed. She had been trying to reach Missy for a couple of days with no success. Not only was Missy her best link to the familiar life back home, she was also her primary link to her grandmother, better known as Nans, who didn't trust computers or cell phones or just about anything else invented after 1942. Nans wasn't even too crazy about push-button phones, though Star had reached her the day before just to let her know that she was all right and that the tour was going well.

"Still can't get through, hmm?" Lola asked sympathetically as her fingers quickly and skillfully unwove Star's hair from the curlers.

Star shook her head. "Guess I'll have to try again later."

13

A little over half an hour later Star was back on the comfortable sofa reading about Hadrian's Wall when there was another knock on the door. This time it was a harried-looking assistant stage manager telling them that Star was due onstage in five minutes.

"Up the stairs, turn left, and down the hall to the red door," the young man said. At least that was what Star thought he said – his heavy Cockney accent and the speed at which the words tumbled out of his mouth made it difficult to tell for sure.

Luckily, though, Mike had scouted the site as soon as they'd arrived and knew exactly where to go. After allowing Lola a few final seconds to touch up Star's pink lip gloss and fluff up her hair, Mike put a hand on Star's shoulder.

"Ready to go, sweetheart?" he asked.

Star nodded, mentally reviewing the opening lyrics to the song she was scheduled to sing. "I'm ready," she replied.

Mike led her out of the dressing room and upstairs to the stage door. He accompanied her into the backstage area, then handed her off to another assistant stage manager, who helped her put on and adjust her microphone headset and then showed her where to wait for her cue.

When the stage manager nodded at her a few minutes later, Star took a deep breath and stepped onto the stage. She rarely got truly nervous before performances, though she always felt a ripple of jittery excitement in her stomach.

The lights onstage were bright, though not as bright as the ones she was used to at her concerts. Reminding herself not to squint, she stepped forward and waved one hand at the crowd she knew was out there beyond the footlights. "Hello, London!" she cried.

A wild, clamorous cheer went up from the audience. Star grinned, her sleepiness forgotten as fresh energy and enthusiasm flooded through her. She glanced over her shoulder at her band. The musicians and backup dancers had come onstage before her and were standing there ready to go. She recognized the round, cheerful face of her band leader, Johnny Shock, and grinned at him. He winked at her in response, his right hand poised over the strings of his electric guitar.

Star turned back to face the audience. "It's great to be here tonight to help you guys honour the most awesome British bands ever," she said. "Now I'd like to sing something for you

– it's my latest release, and it's called 'Always Dreamin'.'"

Right on cue her band swung into the opening chords of the song.

Star was still feeling pumped up and happy as she waved to the audience one last time. The performance had gone so well that Star almost wished she could just signal for the next song on her usual playlist and keep going. But she knew she would have to wait a few days for that, until the first of her two scheduled concerts in Edinburgh.

Mike was waiting for her in the wings. He smiled and held out his arms for a hug as she ripped off her headset and raced towards him.

"Good job, sweetheart," he said. "That audience was eatin' you up like honey from a spoon."

"Thanks." Star hugged him tightly. As the adrenaline from the performance left her, she suddenly felt drained. "I can't wait to get back to our hotel and get some sleep," she added.

Mike gave her a sympathetic look. "Sorry, darlin'," he said. "That'll have to wait a bit more. They'll be expecting you at the after party, remember?"

"Oh, right."

Star's shoulders slumped as she realized that her evening wasn't over. There was going to be a big, splashy party in the hotel ballroom directly after the awards show ended. Star normally had fun at such events, and she knew that it was important to make an appearance at them – the major media outlets would be there covering the party, and the resulting publicity would help sell CDs and concert tickets all over the world. That night, though, she couldn't help wishing that she could skip out on her celebrity duties just for once. But Mike and her whole team had worked hard to get her where she was today, and she wasn't going to let them down just because she was a little tired.

She followed as Mike led the way through the maze of cables, cameras, and other equipment backstage, heading towards the exit door. Behind her Star could hear a presenter announcing the next award.

As they pushed through the door into the quiet hallway beyond, they almost walked into a man standing right on the other side.

"Hey, watch it," the man snarled.

Star stared at him, surprised by the anger in his voice.

The man had an American accent and was medium height and stocky, with pockmarked pale skin and thin black hair slicked back from his broad forehead.

The stranger's small, watery pale blue eyes swept over her and settled on Mike. "Mosley," the man said, spitting out the name like it was a foul-tasting bug that had just flown into his mouth. "I heard you were going to be here."

"Nice to see you, too, Starkey," Mike responded, though judging from the cool tone of his voice he didn't really think it was very nice to see him at all.

Star cast her manager a curious glance. Mike didn't meet her gaze. He was still staring coldly at the stranger. It was obvious that they knew each other, though Star had never seen the other man before as far as she could remember. Who was he? It was obvious that Mike had no intention of introducing them.

"Hi," she said after a moment of tense silence, deciding to take matters into her own hands. She flashed her most winning smile at the stranger. "I'm Star Calloway."

"I know who you are," the man – Starkey – said shortly. "Just another pop wanna-be hogging the limelight from more talented acts."

"That's enough," Mike said sternly as Star blinked in

shock. He grabbed Star's arm and steered her past the other man. Somehow he managed to bump Starkey hard with his shoulder as he passed.

Starkey grunted angrily. "Watch it, Mosley," he snarled. "You don't want any trouble from me, trust me."

"If you don't want trouble, best not to go hollerin' for it," Mike returned icily. "Come on, Star, we're out of here."

Star felt a little shaken as she allowed Mike to drag her off down the hallway. As soon as they turned a corner out of the man's sight, she spun around to face her manager.

"What was that all about?" she demanded, pulling her arm free from Mike's grip, which had become almost painfully firm. She rubbed her elbow and stared at him. "Who was that guy, and why did he say such rude stuff to me? I mean, I don't even know him!"

Mike sighed and rubbed his forehead. "Sorry you had to deal with that, darlin'," he said gruffly. "That's Stan Starkey. You've heard of him, haven't you?"

"Stan Starkey . . . Isn't he that guy who discovered the Winter Kidz a couple of years ago?" Star said, suddenly realizing why the man's last name had sounded familiar. "Hmm, I wonder what ever happened to them . . . Anyway, I think he manages Jade now, right?"

Mike nodded. "Those are the latest," he said. "Starkey's been in the business a long time – long as I have or longer. He's made a fortune promoting all kinds of flash-in-the-pan kiddie pop and short-lived boy bands like the Winter Kidz. He always drops them as soon as they get too old or too cold, though. Most of 'em don't go beyond two albums, if they get that far."

Star was surprised. "But Jade is super-hot," she said. "And she's really talented. She doesn't seem like a flash in the pan to me."

"She *is* talented," Mike agreed. "With a different management team she'd go far. With Starkey?" He shrugged. "Who knows."

Star glanced back down the hall. "But why was he so harsh to us just now?" she asked. "I don't even know him."

"Doesn't matter," Mike said. "I reckon he's as worked up as a dog at a cat show because you got asked to perform tonight and Jade just got to be a presenter. Stuff like that really sticks in his craw."

"Wow." Star shuddered as she thought once again of the ugly expression on Stan Starkey's face. What would it be like to have someone like that as a manager? She couldn't imagine it, and wasn't sure she even wanted to try.

Two

Star leaned against a pillar, willing herself not to rub her tired eyes and smudge the light, natural-looking make-up Lola had so carefully applied before the party. The majestic, high-ceilinged main ballroom at the Londonia Hotel was crammed full of glamourous, attractive, well-dressed people, most of them busy eating and drinking too much and talking too loudly. The mass of people had overwhelmed the air-conditioning, making the huge room feel hot and stuffy, and Star had long since slipped off her stylish pink satin dress's matching jacket and slung it over one arm.

She glanced around wearily, grateful for the moment of peace from the mobs of fans, supporters, and reporters that had been keeping her busy since her arrival. Mike, Tank, and Lola were somewhere in the crowd – Tank had just left to fetch them all sodas from the bar at the far end of the room, and when the crowd shifted just right she could see Mike a few yards away chatting with several important-looking men in tuxedos. Lola had disappeared some time ago, and Star hoped she wasn't gushing too much to the many reporters at the party. Star wasn't wearing a watch, so she could only wonder what time it was and how much longer the gala would go on. She had already spent what felt like days smiling at strangers, answering reporters' questions, and generally trying to pretend she was having fun.

Most people would do anything to trade places with me right now, Star reminded herself, trying to head off her bout of weary self pity. *It's not like hanging at a fancy party eating fabulous food and rubbing elbows with all kinds of celebrities is exactly torture, even if I'm too tired to appreciate it.*

Still, she couldn't help feeling a little cranky as she noticed a petite, attractive woman in a blue gown striding towards her. Star didn't recognize the woman, but the small tape recorder she was holding in one carefully manicured hand made it obvious that she was a reporter.

"Hello, Star," the woman called as she approached, sticking out her free hand. "Nice to meet you. I'm Julia Canterbury from the London *Chat.*"

Star smiled politely, shifting her jacket to her other arm in order to shake the woman's hand. The London *Chat* was one of the newspapers in the stack that was delivered to her hotel suite daily. "Nice to meet you, too," she said.

"I hope you're having a smashing time here in London," the reporter said pleasantly. "Would you mind if I asked you a few questions?"

"Of course not." Star smiled, resigning herself to yet another interview. "Go ahead."

The reporter's first few questions involved Star's new album and tour, and Star easily reeled off her usual responses. She had answered the same questions so many times that she could have done it in her sleep.

"Now, Star." Julia Canterbury took a half-step closer and peered into Star's face. "I understand that you're an orphan, raised by your gran. Would you like to talk about that a bit?"

Star gulped, taken by surprise by the sudden change of topic. As many times as her family history had come up in interviews, as carefully as Mike had coached her on what to say, she was never quite prepared when it happened.

"Nans is awesome," she said, forcing herself to smile.

"She still lives in my hometown in Pennsylvania, and it's really great being able to go home to her and feel like a regular kid again. She's totally been my rock since I was a child."

Julia Canterbury nodded along with Star's words, the flashy gold earrings she was wearing bobbing up and down. "I see," she said. "And your mum and dad – do you mind telling me what happened to them? I wouldn't ask, but I'm afraid I wasn't able to find the answer in my research . . ."

Star took a deep breath. She hated lying, and she especially hating lying about her family – pretending that they didn't exist. That they weren't still out there somewhere. But Mike had convinced her that it was easier this way. Together, they had worked out what to say when the topic came up, and Star had practised until she could reel off her invented family background without hesitation.

Still, whenever possible she preferred to avoid such questions rather than answer them. "I – I'd rather not talk about that," she said, flashing the reporter a wan, apologetic smile. "Do you mind if we change the subject?"

Luckily her natural charm worked on Julia Canterbury just as it had on countless reporters in the past. The woman tut-tutted sympathetically and reached out to pat Star on the arm.

"So sorry, luv," she said. "I certainly didn't mean to upset you. Why don't we go back to talking about music?"

"That sounds great." Star did her best to hide her relief.

"All right then," the reporter said. "Star, my readers are simply mad for young American artists lately. We ran a poll not long ago, and you came out the favourite. Second place was Eddie Urbane. I was hoping to speak with him tonight, but I understand he turned down the Yobbies' invite to sing on the show. As a fellow American star, can you tell me anything about him?"

"He's very talented," Star replied truthfully. "I don't know him personally, though."

"Really?" The reporter sounded surprised. "But I thought the two of you recently appeared on a chat show together. Didn't see it myself, of course, but there was a bit on PopTV about it, I believe."

"Oh. Right." Star winced. She should have known by now that most reporters seemed to know more about her life than she did herself. "I meant to say I've met him a couple of times but I, er, don't know him well." She was careful to keep her tone pleasant. Eddie Urbane was only a few years older than Star, but he'd been in the music business for years. Although she'd always liked his music, he wasn't one of her favourite people at the moment. Just before leaving for England, she'd discovered that Eddie was trying to sabotage her tour. He'd even stooped so low as to dognap Dudley. But Star hadn't said a word to anyone outside her own team about the incident.

When you can't say something nice, don't say anything at all, Star thought, recalling one of her mother's favourite sayings.

Luckily Julia Canterbury seemed satisfied with Star's comments about Eddie. "Third place in our poll went to Jade," she said. "Anything to say about her? I understand she's doing quite well on the American charts as well."

Star glanced around, realizing that she hadn't seen her fellow teen pop princess at the party. "I've never met Jade," she said. "So I don't know much about her except that I really like her first album." Her mind flashed back to her recent unpleasant encounter with Stan Starkey, and Mike's comments afterward. "I guess we'll have to wait and see what happens next."

"Star!" a familiar voice rang out from nearby. "There

you are. I've been looking all over for you."

Star glanced up to see Mike hurrying towards her. He looked extra tall, extra handsome, and a little strange wearing a tuxedo instead of his usual jeans, with his bushy mustache tamed by a dab of Lola's styling gel. His purple cowboy boots, however, were still poking out from the cuffs of his neatly pressed trousers.

"Well, howdy," he said as he joined them, with a charming smile for the reporter. "What are y'all talkin' about over here?"

Within seconds he had made an excuse to pull Star away from the reporter. Julia Canterbury seemed disappointed, but she thanked Star politely and headed towards the bar.

"That's the entertainment writer from one of those London tabloid papers, isn't it?" Mike said as he and Star wandered away in the opposite direction. "Canterbury, right? What was she asking you?"

Star shrugged. "The usual," she said, impressed as always with Mike's seemingly photographic memory for names and faces. "The tour, the album, the whole shebang. Oh, but she did ask a few questions about, you know, my family."

"Oh?" Mike raised one eyebrow.

"Don't worry," Star said quickly. "I just said a few nice things about Nans, then changed the subject as soon as I could."

Mike nodded. "Good girl," he said softly, squeezing her shoulder. "Sorry I wasn't there to help."

"It's okay." Star smiled up at him. "But thanks."

They were approaching a linen-draped table loaded with all sorts of food, along with baskets of free CDs and several huge vats of cut flowers. As Mike stopped to chat with someone, Star continued towards the table, scanning the food selection. She was always hungry after a performance, even a short one, and the sandwich she'd wolfed down while changing clothes for the party hadn't done the trick.

She was heading for a platter of cookies at one end of the table when she spotted a bowl of hard pretzel bits. *Ooh, Dudley loves those!* she thought. She wished the little dog was with her, but Mike had insisted on sending him back to the hotel before the party started. Realizing she was still holding her jacket, Star grabbed a handful of pretzel bits and slipped them into one of the jacket's roomy pockets, hoping they wouldn't fall out in the limo on the way home – Mike was always on her case about Dudley's ever-increasing weight.

She spotted some baby carrots and stuck them into the other jacket pocket, figuring they would be a nice healthy addition to the dog's treat. As she did, her hand bumped something hard and slightly slimy. Pulling out the mystery object, she found herself holding Dudley's favourite plastic bone.

Uh oh, Star thought, tucking it back into the pocket. *Hope the Dudster isn't missing this too much.*

That particular plastic bone had always been one of Dudley's favourite toys. But ever since the tour had started a week earlier, the little dog seemed obsessed with it. Lola had theorized that the bone was a sort of security blanket for him – now that he was so far from home, he didn't want to let it out of his sight.

Star smiled, touching her star necklace with her free hand. She could understand wanting to have something familiar around as a reminder of home.

Half an hour later, as she listened to a bunch of British record executives try to convince Mike to enter some sort of complicated and boring business deal with their company, Star's face was starting to go numb from the cheerful smile she'd pasted on it. Finally she wasn't sure she could stand it anymore.

"Excuse me," she broke in, tugging on Mike's jacket sleeve. She tossed a brilliant smile at the executives. "I'm so sorry to interrupt, but I need to powder my nose. Will you excuse me, please?"

"Of course," one of the men answered, while the others nodded politely.

Mike winked at her. "I'll catch up with you in a little while," he said.

Star hurried towards the closest ladies' room. She was almost there when, out of the corner of her eye, she saw a reporter bearing down on her. Pretending not to see him, she put on an extra burst of speed and dashed through the swinging door.

"Yo!" an annoyed voice greeted her. "Heads up, okay?"

"Oh! Sorry," Star said breathlessly, realizing she'd almost crashed into someone standing at the sink just beyond the doorway.

Then she did a double take as she recognized the face staring at her in the mirror over the sink. The dark hair, the pretty pout, the greenish hazel eyes . . .

"Hey! You're Jade, aren't you?" Star blurted out.

"Got it in one," the other girl said flatly, raising the lip gloss she was holding, and leaning forward towards the mirror. Her gaze barely flickered towards Star before returning to her own reflection.

Star couldn't help noticing that Jade didn't exactly seem thrilled to meet her. Still, even though she was a big star herself, Star was also a fan and always got excited about meeting other celebrities.

"Well, hi," she said. "It's nice to finally meet you. I really love your work. Oh, I'm Star Calloway, by the way."

"I know." Once again Jade's striking eyes darted towards her for a split second.

Feeling awkward because of the other girl's curt response, Star cast around for something else to say. "So, this is a pretty nice place, huh?" she commented lamely, gesturing at their surroundings.

The bathroom was small but luxurious, decorated like some kind of Arabian luxury spa. Billowing purple and gold fabric was draped across the ceiling to form a tentlike canopy, the wallpaper featured exotic patterns, framed paintings of palm trees hung here and there, and the taps on the marble sinks were gleaming gold. In the open space across from the sinks was a cosy seating area featuring several overstuffed chairs on a Persian rug. The toilet area, visible immediately beyond the plump armchairs, looked more normal, though there was another palm tree picture hanging at the end of the aisle. Aside from the two girls, the bathroom seemed to be empty.

Jade merely shrugged. "It's sort of over the top," she said. "This whole hotel is like that. My suite is decorated like some crazy African safari. I'm talking zebra-print carpets, okay?"

"Really?" Star replied, laughing. "So your team is staying here at the Londonia, huh? We're at the Royal Mark a few blocks over."

"Oh yeah?"

Star smiled. Was it her imagination, or were Jade's brief responses sounding a tiny bit friendlier?

She perched on the arm of one of the overstuffed chairs, laying her jacket across her lap. Meanwhile Jade tossed her lip gloss into a beaded handbag that matched the beaded fabric of her strapless dress. Digging into the bag, she grabbed a tube of mascara and unscrewed the top.

"So, is this your first time in London?" Star asked. "How long are you going to be here?"

Jade glanced at her in the mirror. "You ask a lot of questions," she commented, leaning forward to dab at her long eyelashes with the mascara wand. Then she smiled slightly. "But yeah. It's my first time here. My parents don't travel."

"Really?" Star's smile faltered as her hand crept to her star necklace. Her own parents had loved to travel.

"Anyway, it seems pretty cool here," Jade went on, not noticing Star's moment of consternation. "Good thing, too, 'cuz I'm stuck here for like another week. I'm supposed to do a load of interviews and stuff. Colour me bored, you know?"

Star nodded understandingly. "Interviews can be a drag sometimes. But I guess it's all necessary. It pays the bills – that's what my manager Mike always says."

"Yeah. Anyway, as long as I can get some shopping in, it's all good." Jade laughed and shot Star an almost friendly glance as she capped her mascara.

"I like shopping, too," Star replied, eager to keep the conversation going now that Jade seemed to be loosening up a little. "But I'm always happy as long as I can sing something. That always gets me back on track even if I'm in the middle of some kind of press snoozefest, you know?"

Jade shrugged. "I guess."

Star smiled, thinking back to her performance earlier that evening. "I mean, it's all about the music, right?" she mused. "Oh, that reminds me – I'm sure you've heard this a jillion times, but I just have to tell you I totally love 'All Over the Place'. The video is killer, and the song rocks."

Jade grimaced. "Yeah, that's what they tell me," she muttered sourly.

Star was surprised by her reaction. "All Over the Place" had been Jade's first release from her self-titled album and was the song that had rocketed her to stardom.

"What's the matter?" she asked Jade. "Sorry, I didn't mean to upset you or anything."

"No big," Jade said with a sigh. She turned away from the mirror and glanced around the bathroom, which was still empty except for the two of them. "Look, can you keep a secret?"

"Sure!" Star replied instantly. She couldn't help feeling touched that Jade was already willing to confide in her.

"You can't tell anyone," Jade said warningly. She took a

step towards Star. "I mean it. If you blab, I'm going to be all kinds of mad, okay?"

Star crossed her heart with her finger. "You can trust me, I swear." After all, if anyone could keep a big secret, it was her. Wasn't she keeping the biggest secret in her life from most of the world every moment of every day?

Jade perched on the arm of another chair. She glanced at Star, then stared down at her own hands. "Okay," she said. "Like, I don't know why I'm telling you this, really. But whatever. I have to tell someone, okay?"

"Okay," Star said softly, suddenly a little worried. Jade looked so sombre all of a sudden. What if the secret she was about to reveal was something really bad? The image of an angry Stan Starkey flashed through her mind, and she shuddered. She hoped it wasn't anything *too* terrible.

"It's about that – that *song*," Jade said. " 'All Over the Place'. "

"Yes?" Star said expectantly. "What about it?"

Jade clenched her fists on the fabric of the chair arm. "I *hate* it, okay?" she blurted out. "I totally despised it from the first time I heard it. It practically made me hurl. I didn't want to record it at all, let alone put it out as a single."

Star's jaw dropped. Whatever she'd been expecting Jade

to say, that wasn't it. "Really?" she said. "Why didn't you just pass on it, then?"

Jade glared at her. "Easy for you to say," she snapped. "Your manager is different. It's – it's not that simple for me." She shook her head fiercely. "I'm not even allowed to say how much the stupid song reeks, in case it gets out to the media. Stan says if that happened I'd be on the first bus back to Ohio."

Star was pretty sure that was an exaggeration. The media and Jade's fans wouldn't turn against her just because she admitted to not liking one of her songs. But it was obvious that Jade was really upset by the whole topic, and Star wanted to make her feel better if she could.

"It's okay," she said comfortingly. "I mean, it really stinks that you got stuck with a song you hate and all. But if you think *that's* bad, you should hear *my* secret."

"You have a secret?" Jade looked mildly curious. "What is it?"

Star hesitated, wishing that for once her brain could keep up with her mouth. Why had she brought up her own secret? She hardly knew Jade – why would she consider confiding in her, when she hadn't even told certain people she trusted, like Lola?

Too late now, Star thought, trying not to think about what Mike would say if he found out.

"It's my family," she said. "My parents and my baby brother. See, we were on vacation in Florida a couple of years ago, when I was twelve . . ."

With that, it was as if a tidal wave building up inside her had finally been released. The words tumbled out of her in a rush, faster and faster, describing everything that had happened from that fateful day in Florida onwards. Jade listened silently, her greenish eyes wide with amazement.

"Wow," she said when Star finished. "That's so totally extreme. Are you playing me? I mean, how do you keep it out of the media and stuff?"

"It's not easy," Star admitted. "Early on, Mike decided we should keep it hushed up. Of course, it wasn't much of a problem then − I'd just signed with Flashpoint, and nobody knew who I was yet. After my first album dropped . . ." She shrugged, remembering those wild, fun, overwhelming days just a year earlier. "Well, after that it got a little trickier. It seemed like everyone wanted to interview me. So Mike helped me come up with some things to say whenever I get asked about my family. Mostly I try to change the subject. But when I can't, I say that I lost my parents when I was very young, and that I've lived with my grandmother ever since." She shot Jade a rueful smile. "It's almost sort of true, even."

Jade smiled back sympathetically. "Wow," she said again, looking thoughtful. "That's so harsh, having your family disappear like that."

"I know," Star said, touching her necklace. "It's hard to really enjoy everything I have now because they're not here to enjoy it with me. But Mom and Dad taught me to never give up, and I know we'll all be together again someday."

Jade looked confused. "You mean you think you're going to find them one of these days? Like, stranded on a deserted island or something?"

"Yes," Star said without hesitation. "I know they're out there somewhere. I just have to find them."

She half expected Jade to say something negative. Instead the other girl merely nodded. "That's cool," she said. "Good luck."

"Thanks." Star smiled at her. Jade smiled back.

At that moment the bathroom door crashed open and a pale, wiry, wild-eyed woman raced in, banging into Star's chair so hard that Star went flying off onto her hands and knees in the aisle beyond the sink area. Her jacket flew out of her hands and slid under the door of one of the empty toilet stalls.

The newcomer hardly seemed to notice. She skidded to a stop in front of Jade and planted her bony arms on her hips. "There you are!" she cried in a voice that sounded like tires screeching on asphalt. "We've been looking all over the place for your skinny butt. What's taking you so long in here?"

Jade scowled and jumped to her feet. "Whatever, Manda," she muttered. "I was just talking to someone, okay?"

For the first time the newcomer noticed Star sprawled on the tile floor. "Oh!" she exclaimed, smoothing down the front of her black silk dress and patting her close-cropped platinum hair. "So sorry, didn't see you there. It's Star Calloway, isn't it? You look beautiful tonight, honey. So nice to meet you. I'm Manda Smith – I work for Stan Starkey; I'm sure you must be familiar with him . . ."

Star smiled politely, climbing to her feet as the woman rambled on. "Hello," she said. "I'm sorry I kept Jade so long. I'm such a big fan of hers, I just had to talk to her."

"Oh!" Manda glanced over at Jade, seeming uncertain whether to scowl at her or smile back at Star. She settled on an odd sort of half-smirk. "Well, that's all kinds of sweet. But come on, Jade, let's motor. Stan's waiting."

Jade didn't have time to do more than toss a half-irritated, half-apologetic glance in Star's direction as Manda yanked her towards the door. A second later they were gone.

Star pushed through the nearest stall door, then leaned over and grabbed her jacket, which was crumpled against the base of a toilet along with several of Dudley's carrot sticks that had scattered on the floor. Draping the jacket over one arm, she headed for the sink to check her hair and make-up, suddenly very grateful for her own amazing, close-knit team.

Just think, if Mike hadn't found me first, I might've ended up with Stan Starkey and Manda What's-her-name instead, she thought with a shudder as she quickly slicked on a fresh layer of lip gloss.

Staring at her own reflection in the mirror, she felt a flash of pity for Jade. Suddenly, hanging out at the party with Mike and the others for another hour or two, tired or not, didn't seem all that bad.

Three

"Good morning, Dudley," Star said with a giggle, opening her eyes and staring directly into the little dog's round, googly-eyed face. She quickly closed her eyes again, expecting the dog to slurp her from chin to forehead in his usual morning greeting. Instead he stepped off of her stomach, and she heard a soft *thump* as he jumped to the hotel room's carpeted floor. A moment later came the *click-click* of his nails on the parquet floor of the hallway outside her room.

Star opened her eyes again and sat up just in time to see Dudley's curly tail disappear around the bedroom door, which was slightly ajar. She shrugged, then pushed back her covers and stretched. Glancing at the clock on the bedside table, she saw that it was after two in the afternoon.

"Wow," she murmured. No wonder she felt well rested for the first time since the start of the tour. She'd slept for almost twelve hours!

She got out of bed, grabbed the pink cotton robe slung over a nearby chair, and pulled it on over her matching pink-and-silver star-patterned pyjamas. Then she padded out of the bedroom in her bare feet.

There was no sign of life in the suite's central sitting room, though several packed trunks and suitcases were stacked near the door. A quick peek into the other bedrooms where Mike, Tank, Mags, and Lola were staying showed that she was the only person in the suite. She glanced around the main room, which was tastefully decorated in shades of burgundy and beige, with sturdy English antique furniture and framed oil paintings on the walls. After only a week it had already started to feel like home. Star wondered what their next accommodations would be like.

Suddenly she noticed Dudley sitting by the front door. He was staring up at the knob intently.

"What's wrong, Dudley?" Star asked. "Do you need to go out?"

Instead of barking at the word *out* as he often did, Dudley ignored her. He turned away from the door and hurried across the room, not even glancing in her direction.

"Don't be mad, Dudley," Star called after him as he headed down the hallway towards her bedroom. "I *had* to shut you out of my room last night – you kept wriggling and waking me up."

The little dog kept going. Star shrugged. Obviously she wasn't the only one having trouble adjusting to their new travel schedule. Dudley had been so restless the night before that she'd finally given up on getting any sleep with him there and tossed him out into the hall, though someone had obviously let him in with her again some-time that morning.

Her stomach grumbled loudly, and she wandered over to the round cherry table that served as a dining area, hoping to find a banana or a box of doughnuts. Instead she saw a note on the table in Mike's familiar scrawl.

Star,

We had to go out to take care of some details. Order yourself some room service for break-fast and then get yourself packed. We leave at four. (Tank already walked the dog.)

M.

Below that was another note, this one in Mags's crisp, concise handwriting.

> *P.S. Star, I hope you finished the book on Hadrian's Wall. We'll be seeing the wall from the bus this afternoon, and I want you to be ready to tell me all about it.*

Star grimaced. She'd barely read two chapters in the history book.

"Oh, well," she said aloud. "At least I can do one thing in this note."

Picking up the phone on the table, she dialled room service and ordered juice, toast, and scrambled eggs with bacon. She also requested an extra side plate of bacon for Dudley, hoping to make amends.

While she waited for her food to arrive, Star grabbed the stack of newspapers someone had left on one of the chairs. *I can't face Hadrian before breakfast,* she thought as she sat down at the table with the papers in front of her.

The London *Chat* was on the top of the pile. Star flipped through it aimlessly until she reached the entertainment pages. A picture of herself took up almost a third of the first page. Below that, in huge type, the headline screamed STAR CALLOWAY EXCLUSIVE! Smaller type below the headline added, "Hear what this superstar singer has to say about life, love, and luck. By Julia Canterbury."

"I don't remember talking to her about life, love, and luck," Star murmured, rolling her eyes. Though it had happened before, she couldn't help being shocked every time a reporter embellished or made up things while writing about her. She scanned the article, finding it mostly the same old information that appeared in almost every article about her, along with a couple of quotes from the short interview she'd given at the party.

But a paragraph near the end caught her eye. She blinked, rereading it.

Naturally this teen diva regularly rubs shoulders with the best in the biz. Star had only the most brilliant things to say to this reporter about yummy young Yankee heartthrob Eddie Urbane. But when queried about her fellow American pop princess, Star seemed a bit more cagey.

"Jade has made one decent album, but we'll have to

wait and see," Star said with an unreadable expression. "Her next one could be fabulous – or a flop."

Could this be a rivalry in the making? So far there's a clear Star rising on the charts, but look out, Calloway – Jade is coming on strong! In any case, this reporter doesn't care who wins the title of supreme singing superstar from across the pond, as long as both artists continue making fab music that keeps us all dancing.

Star frowned at the paper, irritated. "I didn't say anything like that!" she said to Dudley, who had just reappeared at the end of the hallway. "I said I didn't know her, I liked her album, and I wanted to see what she did next. Or something like that."

She wrinkled her brow, trying to remember her exact words. As she was thinking, there was a knock on the door. Dudley let out a halfhearted bark, then flopped down onto the floor near the table, looking grumpy.

"That was fast," Star said, hurrying to let in the room service person, a young woman with short reddish-blonde hair.

"Your breakfast, miss," the server said politely in a crisp, cultured British accent as she pushed a food-laden cart into the room.

"Thanks." Star stepped out of the way as the young woman bustled around the table, carefully setting out food, linens, and cutlery. She even set the vase of fresh flowers from her cart beside Star's plate. Finally she stood back.

"Will there be anything else, miss?"

"No, thank you," Star said politely. She hurried over to the small table near the door, where Mike left a few smaller bills to use as tips for the hotel staff. "Here you go. Thanks a bunch!"

The server waved away the money Star was offering. "No, no," she said. "It – it was truly an honour to serve you." Her cheeks turned pink, and she glanced behind her at the half-open door to the hall. "Listen, Miss Calloway, I'm not supposed to say this, but I'm a huge fan of yours! I saw your concert on Wednesday night, and you were super!"

Star grinned. "Thanks! I'm glad you had fun."

The young woman smiled back. "Listen, don't tell me boss, will you?" she said, her cultured tones slipping into a more casual Cockney accent. "But I'd absolutely love an autograph. If you don't mind, that is."

"I can do better than that." Star hurried over to the coffee table across the room. There was a messy pile of promotional materials there – CDs, glossy photos, a few tour posters, and more. Star selected a poster and hurried back to the young server. "Here, I can sign this for you. Okay?"

"Brilliant!" the young woman said happily. "Cheers, thanks a lot!"

Soon she was wheeling her empty cart out with one hand, clutching her souvenir with the other. Star waved as the young woman shut the door. Then she glanced at Dudley as she sat down to eat. She was surprised that the little dog had hardly paid any attention to the stranger while she was in the room; usually he was so friendly that he made a pest of himself. Star hoped he wasn't getting sick. But when she set the plate of bacon she had ordered for him on the floor, he scarfed it down as eagerly as ever, which made her feel a little better.

Just as Dudley finished licking the bacon plate, the door opened and Mike walked in.

"What's that dog eating?" he asked immediately.

Star grinned sheepishly. "Nothing?" she tried hopefully.

Mike frowned at her. "Star, if you keep feeding that beast twenty meals a day, he's going to look more like a pig than a pug."

Star decided it was time to change the subject. She grabbed the London *Chat* and held it up. "Did you see this?" she asked. "That reporter from last night totally misquoted me!"

"Let me see." Mike took the paper and scanned the article. "Hmm," he said when he finished. "Interesting."

"What do you think?" Star asked anxiously. "It sounds like I was insulting Jade, and I definitely wasn't. I hadn't even met her yet when I said that stuff. I hope she doesn't get upset if she sees it."

Mike scowled as he reread the end of the article. But then he glanced at Star, shrugged, and tossed the paper back on the pile with the others. "Don't pay any attention to what that rag says," he told her. "Nobody else does. It's just a minor local tabloid – there're probably more guests in this hotel right now than people who pay the *Chat* any mind."

Star smiled, relieved. "Good," she said, pushing back from the table. "Okay, then unless you need me for something, I'd better go pack. Scotland, here we come!"

Star stepped out of the hotel lobby at five minutes after four with Dudley's leash in one hand and her pink duffel bag in the other. Her tour bus was already idling at the curb, and

Tank immediately ushered her towards it with the help of several of the hotel's security guards. A few fans and photographers were clustered on the sidewalk nearby, but luckily the news of their departure hadn't spread too much.

"Hi, everyone!" Star called to the small crowd, shifting her bag to the same hand as the leash so she could wave. "Thanks for making me feel so welcome in London. Now wish me luck in Scotland!"

She climbed up the bus steps to the sound of her fans' answering cheers. Once inside, she dropped her duffel in the rack behind the driver's seat and headed back to the main area of the bus. The tour bus was meant to be the whole team's home away from home, and while the outside looked like nothing more than an ordinary luxury charter bus, the customized interior had been outfitted with comfort and convenience in mind. Most of its length had been turned into a sort of rolling living room, with several seating areas and a complete entertainment system. Behind that a small but well-stocked kitchenette with a built-in table and banquettes served as Star's school desk as well as a dining table for the whole crew. The back end of the bus contained several smaller rooms – a fully equipped bathroom, several tiny but cosy bunks for napping, and a small office with a phone and computer.

Lola was already sitting at the narrow table filing her nails when Star boarded. "Good morning, babydoll," the stylist greeted her with a smile. "Glad to see you up and about before sundown."

Star giggled. "Hey, I'm a growing girl. I need my sleep, right?"

She kneeled down on the carpeted floor and snapped off Dudley's leash. The little dog immediately headed for the open door.

"Hey!" Star exclaimed, surprised. She jumped forward and grabbed him by the collar just in time to stop him from leaping down the steps onto the sidewalk. The little dog wriggled in her arms as she carried him back inside. "What's up with you? I thought you loved riding in the bus."

Lola shrugged. "Hope he's not sick of travelling already," she said. "We've got a lot of miles to go in this thing before the tour's over."

Star patted Dudley on his round head. "He'll get used to it. I'm sure of it. Meanwhile I guess I'll just have to keep the leash on until the doors are shut."

Before long Mike and Mags joined them. A second later Tank leaped up the steps and looked around.

"Everyone aboard who's coming aboard?" he asked.

Mike nodded. "Let's roll."

"Okay." Tank sat down in the driver's seat and strapped himself in. *"Vamanos!"*

Soon they were rolling down the busy streets of London at the head of a procession of matching buses. There were several separate buses for the musicians, dancers, roadies, and various others who travelled with Star, while most of the equipment followed in tractor trailers. The publicists, accountants, and miscellaneous business types Mike had hired for the tour usually travelled separately in their own vehicles or by plane or train.

Star flopped onto the long couch built into one wall beneath a row of windows and glanced outside. The windows were tinted so that no one could see in, but she could easily see out. Most of the people on the streets were going about their business, though she saw a few people here and there who stopped to gawk at the passing tour bus parade.

She smiled as she spotted a gaggle of preteen girls standing at a bus stop. Once upon a time she would have been just like them – pointing to the buses, speculating about which musician or movie star might be behind that tinted glass. Had any of the girls been to one of her concerts? She wished there was a way to find out, but the thought had hardly formed before the bus had whooshed past and they were out of sight.

"Star," Mags said, interrupting her thoughts, "are you prepared to talk about Hadrian's Wall now?"

Star winced. "Sorry, Mrs Nattle," she said. "I didn't quite finish the book last night." She knew better than to make any excuses, like the performance on the awards show or the party afterward. She already knew what Mags would say to that: *Even rock stars need to learn world history.*

Star shivered and wrapped her arms around herself as she stepped out of the bus in Edinburgh. Despite the fact that it was June, the evening air was chilly and damp. A cool, ghostly mist hung in the air, obscuring the view of the upper floors of their hotel, which appeared to be one of the taller buildings in that part of town.

"So this is Edinburgh," Star murmured, more to herself than to anyone else. She glanced around curiously, taking in the cobblestone streets and the distant view of the craggy, fog-shrouded stone visage of Edinburgh Castle overlooking quaint old cottages and modern storefronts alike.

She took a deep breath of the cool, damp air, which smelled faintly of wood smoke and wet grass. The seven-hour trip from London had been interesting and enjoyable. Even Mags had seemed so awed by the gorgeous scenery of the English and Scottish countryside that she'd forgiven Star for slacking off on her homework. Instead the two of them had discussed British geography and history, Hadrian's Wall, and many other topics that seemed much too interesting to be school subjects. Tank had joined in a few times from the driver's seat, adding the perspective he'd gained from travelling around the world numerous times and learning at least a smattering of words in fifteen or twenty foreign languages. Star was pretty sure she ended up learning more than she ever would have sitting in a stuffy classroom back in New Limpet, and was once again reminded how lucky she was.

The only thing that kept the trip from being perfectly pleasant was Dudley. Star glanced at the little dog as he jumped off the bus beside her and glared at a small bird hopping around in a hedge nearby. He was still acting strange –

cranky, distracted, and just plain not himself – and Star was beginning to worry. The adults seemed convinced that it was just all the travelling, but Star wasn't so sure. The only real travelling they'd done so far was the flight to London, the tour bus ride from the airport, and then a few trips around town in a hired car. That was certainly no worse than many trips on which he'd accompanied Star out to Los Angeles or other spots around the United States.

She did her best to put her worry out of her mind as she followed the others inside. Mike had called ahead to let the hotel know when they were almost there, and they were whisked upstairs to their suite immediately.

"This is nice," Star commented as she walked into the living area and looked around. The hotel was smaller and less formal than the one in London, but it was comfortably furnished with shabby but attractive upholstered furniture and cosy-looking prints of Scottish scenery. Dudley immediately started sniffing the large potted plant in the entryway, seeming almost like his normal self.

"It's getting late," Mike said, checking his watch as he stepped into the suite. "Let's just order us up a few vittles from room service and call it a night. Tomorrow is a free day – no concert, no press commitments, not even a rehearsal – and we want to be rested enough to enjoy it!"

Star grinned as Lola and Tank let out a hearty cheer, and even Mags joined in with a dignified "Hear, hear!" She knew better than to think that Mike would actually spend the day relaxing, but maybe he'd take at least a few hours off to explore Edinburgh with the rest of them before going back to his phone calls and paperwork.

"So, what are we going to do with all that free time?" she asked. "We'll have to figure out how to cram all the important sights of Edinburgh into one day. Hey, looks like the evening paper just got delivered – maybe we can find some ideas in there."

She picked up the newspaper she'd just spotted lying on the floor in the hallway outside the open suite door. It was the evening edition of one of the big London papers, not a local one, and she was about to toss it aside when a headline near the bottom of the front page caught her eye. She gasped, grasping the paper with both hands and staring in dismay.

"Mike!" she cried. "Look what this says: 'Pop Controversy American Style: Jade Appalled by Star's Cross Comments!'"

Four

Mike rubbed his forehead as he looked over Star's shoulder at the newspaper. "Can't say as I'm surprised," he admitted after a moment.

"What?" Star cried. "What do you mean? I thought you said nobody paid any attention to the *Chat*."

"Call it wishful thinking, darlin'," Mike told her gently. "I was hoping nobody would notice that quote, though I knew if Stan Starkey saw it he'd latch on to it like ugly on an ape. That's his way. Any publicity is good publicity in his book. But it'll be okay – our publicity team is already on alert. I'm only surprised someone hasn't called me yet." He pulled one of his cell phones out of his shirt pocket and glanced at it. "Anyway, don't fret, sweetheart. We'll take care of it."

Star bit her lip and stared at the newspaper in her hands. "But what if Jade thinks I really said those mean things about her?"

After Mike's reassuring words she wasn't really thinking

about the public reaction to the article. After all, if he'd managed to keep her family secret quiet for this long, he shouldn't have any trouble quashing a few rumours about a nonexistent rivalry with Jade. But she definitely didn't want to inadvertently hurt the other singer's feelings. Despite Jade's rather prickly attitude at the beginning of their acquaintance, Star had ended up genuinely liking her.

"Don't worry," Lola said reassuringly. "Mike will make things right. Just you wait and see. He lives for stuff like this."

Despite her worry Star giggled as she realized that Mike was already on the phone with someone, talking in a fast, low voice. "I guess you're right," Star said, deciding to put any worries about Jade out of her mind long enough to give her manager time to fix things. She glanced around the room. "Now, who has the room service menu? I'm starved!"

The next day Star dressed in jeans and a baggy sweater her grandmother had knitted for her, with a rain hat over her distinctive curly blonde hair. She picked up the large sunglasses she always wore when she was trying not to be noticed in public.

"Scotland makes it easy to go incognito," she commented

to Lola, who was looking more subdued and normal than usual herself in a long, dark blue wool dress, with a plaid scarf mostly covering her wildly coloured hair. "No worries about getting hot under layers of disguises, even in June – not in this almost arctic weather." One of the facts that Mags had mentioned the day before was that Edinburgh was at the same latitude as the chilly northern cities of Moscow, Copenhagen, and Hudson Bay, Canada.

Lola chuckled. "Way to look on the bright side, baby-doll," she said. "But it does make your sunglasses look a tad wacky. This place isn't exactly the Riviera."

With a glance out the window, Star had to agree. The morning sky was gloomy, with layers of threatening steel grey clouds gathering over the distant hills. Despite the weather, Star was feeling sunny and chipper. She'd had another good night's sleep and had decided to take Lola's advice and let Mike worry about the press. Even Dudley seemed to be more himself that morning, though Star had reluctantly decided to leave him in the suite to rest just in case he was coming down with something.

"So, where are we going first?" she asked Lola, leaning over to pull on a pair of sneakers.

"Wherever you want," Lola said. "I'm supposed to turn you over to Mags after lunch for study time at the castle – guess it's some sort of historical treasure or whatnot. Until then you and Tank and I are on our own." She grinned, putting on an accent that was probably supposed to sound Scottish, though it was more like a mix between the BBC and the Bronx. "Fancy a bit of shopping?"

Star grinned back. "Always!"

"Are you two almost finished?" Tank asked wearily.

"In a minute . . ." Star held up a brightly coloured plaid kilt, eyeing it carefully to see whether it would fit Missy. Deciding it was close enough, she turned around and handed it to the shopkeeper. The plump, well-dressed, white-haired man was following her eagerly around his quaint shop, which seemed to sell a little bit of everything Scottish, from sweaters to shortbread.

"I think I'll take this, too, please," Star said.

The shopkeeper took it from her with a slight bow. "Aye, Miss Calloway," he said in a lilting Scottish brogue. "A good choice – that one's of such bonny cloot. I'll put it over here with the lot."

"Thank you." Star was finding the local dialect a bit difficult to understand at times, but even when she didn't know what the words meant she loved the way they sounded – like spoken music. She glanced over at Lola, who was digging through a bin of odds and ends. "See anything else?" she asked the stylist.

"No!" Tank answered for Lola with a groan. "Come on, you've bought everything already. *Àwhinatia au i òku raruraru . . .*"

Star laughed, recognizing one of Tank's favourite Maori expressions of dismay. Tank always complained about accompanying her on shopping trips – and with so many languages at his disposal, his complaints could get very colourful – though she suspected he didn't mind the shopping trips as much as he pretended to. She was tempted to linger a little longer just to tease him, but decided against it. The shopkeeper had closed his store to the public while Star shopped, and she felt a bit guilty about keeping his other customers out any longer than necessary.

"Don't worry, Tank, I think we're almost finished," she said. "Lola?"

"Right with you," the stylist replied distractedly, holding up a pair of tartan-patterned tights. "Hey, Star, check these out – adorable or what? I was thinking you could wear them onstage with a black skirt or something."

"Perfect!" Star exclaimed. "Add them to the pile."

She led the way over to the cash register just inside the shop's bolted glass doors. Lola dropped the tights onto the sizable pile of clothes and souvenirs on the polished marble counter.

"Okay, I think we're ready to check out." Star smiled at the shopkeeper, then glanced over her shoulder at Tank and Lola. "We can drop this stuff at the hotel and still have time for a nice, leisurely lunch before it's time to meet Mrs Nattle."

She waited for Tank to step forward and pay, but he was staring out the front windows. "Tank?" she said. "Come on, you have the credit card, right?"

"Huh?" Tank turned and blinked at her. "Sorry, Star-baby. I was just looking outside – seems like we have a bit of a crowd gathering. Somebody must've heard you were here."

"Oh." Star glanced out the windows. Sure enough, dozens of faces, young and old, were pressed against the glass. Now that she listened, she could hear the faint sounds of screams and whistles as the fans tried to attract her attention.

She waved to them, then stepped out of sight behind a rack of shirts. "Bummer," she said, peeling off her hat. "Guess I won't need my disguise anymore, huh?"

"Don't worry," Tank told her as he handed the shopkeeper a credit card. "I'm sure this place has a back door."

"Oh, but we can't sneak out the back," Star protested. "Those people will be so disappointed. Can't I just go out and sign a few autographs?"

The shopkeeper cleared his throat. Star glanced at him.

"Pardon, lass," the shopkeeper said apologetically. "If yer signing autographs – well, me granddaughter Coira just adores you. She's a sweet bairn, she is – just nine years old, and has been fair gutted because she could nee get tickets to yer concerts . . ."

"Of course!" Star glanced at Tank, who handed her a pen and a publicity postcard from his jacket pocket. She quickly signed the picture, then handed it to the shopkeeper. "Here you go. And now I'd like you to sign something for me. If you'll write down your granddaughter's name and address, I'll have someone come by her house with tickets to my next show."

The shopkeeper gasped. "Och, lassy, are ye serious?" he

exclaimed, his eyes lighting up. "She'll be positively chuffed!"

Meanwhile Tank was looking out the front window again. When he turned to face Star, his expression was grim. "I'm sorry, Star-baby," he said. "I don't think we should risk going out there. The crowd is getting bigger, and there's not a police officer in sight."

Before Star could protest, the shopkeeper cleared his throat again. "Er, if ye like, ye can sign right here in the shop," he said. "Let 'em in a tad at a time – do ye ken? She'll sit there behind the counter, and they'll come to her, one by one."

"Oh, what an awesome idea!" Star cried, clapping her hands. "Thank you so much! That will work, won't it, Tank?"

Tank shrugged. "I suppose it could, if you make sure to stay behind the counter," he said, pulling a cell phone out of his pocket. "Just give me a second to call for backup so we can get out of here when we're finished."

Star massaged her right hand, which was still a little sore from signing hundreds of autographs earlier that day in the shop. Still, she had loved every second of it – meeting her fans was one of her favourite things about being famous. It wasn't until her stomach had started grumbling so loudly that the fans could hear it that Tank finally convinced her it was time to go have their long-delayed lunch. By that time they were already over an hour late meeting Mags, so Lola had ducked into a fast-food place to grab them some burgers while Star waited in the car with Tank.

Now Star, Mags, and Tank were standing in a cold drizzle on a balcony in Edinburgh Castle, looking down at the ancient pet cemetery tucked into a corner courtyard.

"Too bad Dudley's not here to see this," Star commented with a giggle.

Mags glanced at her over the tops of her bifocals. "Good thing," she said. "The way that dog's been acting, he'd probably leap over the balcony or some such thing."

Star opened her mouth to protest, then shut it with a sigh, admitting to herself that Mags was right. Dudley *was* a little unpredictable lately, and he probably would have been a distraction during their tour of the castle. With the help of several friendly, knowledgeable Scottish tour guides, Mags had told Star all about the ancient fortress's long history, from the first inhabitants of the Castle Rock in 850 B.C. through many invasions, sieges, and controversies.

They had climbed up and down winding staircases, visited a Victorian military prison and the apartment of Mary Queen of Scots, seen the Scottish crown jewels, and enjoyed the spectacular view of the city from the castle's walls.

After gazing at the tiny gravestones of the pet cemetery for another moment, the trio moved back inside the castle. Star took off her rain hat and fluffed up her hair with her fingers. Just as she did, a gaggle of teenage girls happened to walk past on the other side of the velvet ropes the guides had set up to keep Star's group separated from the public.

"Och! Look here, girls – it's her! Star Calloway!" one of the teens cried, spotting Star.

"Are you real?" One of the other girls elbowed her way closer and gasped when she saw Star. "It *is* her!"

Star smiled and walked over to them. "Yep, it's me," she said. "How are you?"

The girls just stared at her, openmouthed. None of them seemed to know what to say next. There were about half a dozen of them, most of them a year or two older than Star.

"So," Star said. "Are you guys from Edinburgh? It's such an awesome city – I've just been touring the castle. Do you know any other fun things I should make sure to do while I'm in town?"

"Aye! Fancy coming to our ceilidh tonight?" the boldest of the girls said breathlessly.

"Your cay-what?" Star asked.

The girls all giggled. "Ceilidh," the bold one repeated. "It's a sort of dance, like a party. Should be fair braw! And if ye'll come, we'll nar tell a soul – word of honour!"

"Really? Tell me more," Star said, ignoring Mags's startled look.

The girls were all eager to speak now. They quickly explained that the neighbourood where they all lived was holding the event, which would feature a lot of traditional Scottish dancing and local food. They told Star the time and place as well.

"Sounds like fun," Star told them. "I'll be there if I possibly can. Promise!"

Mags and Tank looked at her in surprise. "Er, hadn't you better check with Mike first?" Mags asked.

"It'll be okay," Star assured her. "I've got the whole day free, remember? And this cay – kie – er – dance thingy sounds like just the way to top it off."

The girls cheered wildly. "See you tonight, then!" they cried as Star waved and moved on to the next room on her tour.

By the time Star, Mags, and Tank stepped out of the castle an hour later the dark storm clouds had drifted off to the horizon, and the pale rays of the afternoon sun were making everything look very green and sparkly. Star was disappointed when Mags announced that it was time to head back to the hotel.

"Oh, but there's so much more to see!" she protested. "We've hardly been anywhere yet."

"If you're really planning to make an appearance at that ceilidh tonight, you'd better get back and start convincing Mike it's a good idea," Mags pointed out in her usual pragmatic manner. "Besides, you've got a concert to do the night after tomorrow, and two full days of interviews and promo recordings before that. You need to rest up. And I'm still expecting you to finish that book on Hadrian's Wall – and write a two-page paper on it by the end of the week."

Star nodded obediently, knowing better than to argue with her tutor. Besides, Mags had a point. The day had been so relaxing that it was easy to forget they all had to go back to work tomorrow.

When they reached the hotel, they found one of the roadies outside walking Dudley. "Hi, Ralphie," Star greeted the tall, muscular man. Then she bent over to pat Dudley.

"You'd better get upstairs," the roadie said by way of greeting. "Mike's been waiting for you to get back."

"What's the matter?" Star asked, noting Ralphie's serious expression.

The roadie merely jerked his head towards the hotel doors. "Mike'll want to tell you himself."

Star rushed inside, not bothering to wait and make sure Tank and Mags were keeping up. At Ralphie's words a vivid image of her parents had flitted through her mind. What if that was why Mike wanted to see her? What if they'd finally been found? For a second she felt a surge of hope. Then she shook her head, trying to bring herself back down to earth.

Ralphie wouldn't look so serious if it was about that, she thought. *He wouldn't even know, if it was about that. Besides, Mike would've called us for something that important.*

Her whole body suddenly seemed to go limp. Of course – Tank always carried a cell phone and a beeper, and Mike wouldn't have hesitated to contact him if he really had that sort of news. Wondering if there was some change in the schedule or something, Star stopped and waited for Mags and Tank to catch up.

When they entered the suite a few minutes later, Mike was pacing back and forth near the door, a phone pressed to his ear. He spotted Star and stopped talking abruptly.

"I'll call you back," he said into the phone. "Star," he said as he hung up. "Bad news, I'm afraid."

"What is it?" Star asked anxiously.

Mike sighed loudly, his mustache quivering. "Seems that innocent little misquote of yours has blown up into a full-scale media war," he said. "Partly thanks to our very own Glenda Gossip here."

He waved a hand, and for the first time Star noticed Lola standing forlornly by the window. "I'm sorry," the stylist wailed. "I didn't mean to cause trouble. I just didn't think before I spoke, I guess."

"What happened?" Star asked, confused.

Mike quickly filled her in. After dropping off Star with Mags, Lola had encountered a cluster of reporters near the hotel. When they'd asked her about the Star-Jade situation,

Lola hadn't been able to resist saying a few words. She'd ended up insisting hotly that Jade should apologize to Star for jumping to the wrong conclusion about that first newspaper article.

"Turned out one of the dudes was from one of the wire services, and soon that little tidbit was out everywhere," Mike went on heavily. "The papers and TV are running with it. As if that weren't enough, Jade's camp released a statement a little while ago – said they think the altitude of that number one spot on the charts is going to your head."

Star winced, dismayed. "But I never said any of the stuff they think I said!" she cried. "I never said anything bad about Jade in the first place. And Lola's the one who said that about apologizing! Why are they blaming me?"

"Sorry, Star," Lola whimpered.

Star glanced at her and forced a smile. "It's all right," she said. "I know you were just trying to defend me." She turned back to Mike. "Now how do we fix this?"

"Leave that to me," Mike said. "We're already working on it. I just wanted you to know exactly what's going on."

Star nodded. She knew that because of her age, Mike protected her from a lot. The lengths he'd gone to in hiding the story about her parents was just one example of that. But she appreciated the way that he trusted her to handle the truth, the whole truth, and nothing but the truth about most aspects of her career.

"Okay, keep me posted," Star said. "Anyway, can we order dinner now? We didn't have much for lunch, and I was invited to a dance tonight – it's okay if I go, right?"

Mike blinked at her in surprise. "You were what?" he asked. When she explained, he shook his head. "Sorry, dar-lin'. I don't think that's a good idea. You'd better stick around the suite tonight – no sense borrowing trouble."

"But Mike!" Star protested. "I don't want to miss out on this – besides, what's the big deal?"

"The big deal is that the press are going to be all over you like ticks on a coonhound."

"I don't care. I want to go," Star said stubbornly. "This could be my only chance in my whole life to go to a real Scottish cay-whatsit dance. Besides, I promised those girls I'd show."

"You promised you'd come *if you possibly could*," Mags corrected.

Star couldn't help feeling a twinge of annoyance at her

tutor's constant insistence on precision. "Okay, okay," she said. "I'm going if I possibly can. And *I* think I possibly can. Please?" She stared at Mike, holding her breath as she waited for his response.

There was a moment of silence as Mike stared at her thoughtfully. "Fine," he said at last. "I reckon you've got your heart set on it, and it's not worth the ulcers to try to change your mind."

Star let out a happy cheer. "Thanks, Mike!" she added. "You're the best!"

Mike rubbed his forehead and sighed. "But I'm coming with you." He glanced at Tank. "Call in a few of the other guys, would you?" he told him, referring to the security guards and larger roadies who sometimes helped with crowd control at Star's public appearances. "Considering everything that's going on, we don't want to take any chances."

Star had only been at the ceilidh for five minutes when she realized she had made a big mistake. While the neighbourood girls and their families and friends seemed genuinely thrilled to see her, the hall was packed with reporters within moments of her arrival. Star had no idea who had tipped them off, but it seemed that every media type in Edinburgh had turned out for the modest little ceilidh. They pushed aside the neighbourood party goers as they jockeyed for position, calling out questions about Jade and trying to snap as many photos of her as possible.

"Sorry, Mike," Star said as she ducked behind him and Tank to hide from a particularly aggressive photographer. "I guess you were right. This was a mistake. We'd better go before the whole ceilidh is ruined." She really hated to leave just when she'd finally learned to pronounce *ceilidh,* but things were getting chaotic because of her presence, and that wasn't fair to her hosts.

Mike grabbed her hand and gave it a quick squeeze. "It's all right, sweetheart," he said kindly. "It was worth a try. Hold tight, and I'll get us gone."

"We're not going to get out of here without her making a statement," Star heard Tank mutter to Mike.

"Don't count on it," Mike murmured back. Then he put a hand on Star's shoulder. "Come on, we're going to move when I say *go,*" he whispered, his mustache tickling her ear. "And you know what to say to any questions, right?"

At her nod he clapped his hands and shouted for attention. "Please stand aside and let us through," he called in his most commanding voice. "Thanks for your cooperation."

Some of the reporters moved aside to let them pass, but others didn't cooperate very well. Every time someone tried to get too close to Star, Tank or one of the other bodyguards was there to stop him or her. Before long Star was outside on the sidewalk breathing in the fresh, cold evening air.

"There's the car," Mike said, pointing to the hired limousine idling by the curb. "Go on, get in."

Star nodded and hurried towards the car. She was still several feet from it when a tall, lanky man jumped out at her from behind another car.

"Star," he barked aggressively in a British accent, shoving the microphone from his handheld tape recorder into her face. "I'm sure you've heard by now that Jade thinks your ego's out of control. What do you have to say about that?"

Star wished she could answer the question sincerely – explain that this was all one big ridiculous misunderstanding, that she had nothing whatsoever against Jade . . . Instead she took a deep breath and glanced at Mike.

"No comment," she said to the reporter, just as Tank leaped forward to push the reporter aside and shepherd Star into the car.

Five

Star sat bolt upright in bed, panting and sweaty palmed. She'd just woken from a bad dream. She didn't remember much of it, though, aside from the fleeting image of something white and hard and smooth, surrounded by the sound of rushing water – and a deep, lingering feeling of hopelessness.

Glancing at the window of her hotel bedroom, she saw that it was morning. She shivered as she pushed back the covers, accidentally tossing them over a sleeping Dudley. The little dog woke up suddenly and barked.

"Quit complaining," Star said grumpily, yanking the covers off him. "Maybe I wouldn't be having bad dreams if you hadn't woken me up ten times last night. Thanks to you, I could probably sleep for another three hours."

She knew that wasn't going to happen. In addition to preparing for the next evening's concert, she was scheduled to do a local radio interview and record a couple of promo spots. After patting Dudley to show she wasn't really mad at him, she pulled on her robe. Then she grabbed her handheld from the dresser, quickly punching in Missy's e-mail address, as she'd done several times over the past couple of days. As usual her message came back undeliverable.

Star sighed and headed out to the main room, which smelled of coffee and fried eggs. Mags, Tank, and Lola were seated around a table eating breakfast, while Mike paced nearby with his cell phone in his hand.

"Ah, Star. There you are," he said when she entered. "I was just going to come wake you up. Listen, there's been a slight change in plans."

"What do you mean?" Star asked with a yawn. She flopped into the vacant chair at the table and helped herself to a piece of toast. She broke off a small piece of buttery crust and looked around for Dudley, who usually begged for a bite of whatever she was eating. But he was nowhere in sight, and she realized he hadn't followed her from the bedroom. She frowned, feeling a flash of worry, and popped the crust into her mouth.

"Star?" Mike said, watching her. "Are you listening?

Because this is important. This rivalry thing with Jade has heated up a bit overnight. And I think it's time to nip it in the bud."

"Huh?" Star blinked as what he was saying sank in. "What are you talking about?"

"We're postponing the interview you were going to do today," Mike said. "I've called a press conference instead. It starts in two hours."

"A press conference?" Star repeated blankly. She was still feeling a little distracted, both by her concern about Dudley and by the persistent melancholy mood left over from that dream. What had that polished white object been, and why had it left her feeling so gloomy?

Tank leaned over and snapped his fingers in front of her face. "Earth to Star," he said jokingly. "You in there, Star-baby?"

"Oh! Sorry," Star said, realizing she was drifting again. She reached over and poured herself a glass of juice from the pitcher on the table, hoping that would wake her up a little. "Okay, so this press conference. What am I supposed to say?"

"We'll go over that right now." Mike tucked his phone in his pocket and sat down at the table. "Basically, we want to clear the air, let everyone know that there are no hard feelings between you and Jade – at least not on your end."

"Good," Star said. "Because that's true. I . . ." Her voice trailed off as Dudley padded into the room, his head hanging low. Even his normally jaunty tail was drooping.

"What's the matter?" Mike asked.

Star pointed. "It's Dudley," she said. "He still doesn't seem quite right."

Mike frowned impatiently at the dog. "He'll be fine."

Maybe it was the lingering effects of that strange dream, but Star wasn't willing to ignore Dudley's weird behaviour anymore. "No, he's really not himself," she said. "Please, can't we take him to a vet or something? He must be sick."

Mike sighed. "If I promise to get a vet over here, will you promise to forget about that dog and focus on this press conference?"

"Of course," Star said with an angelic smile.

"I'll take care of the vet business, Mike," Mags said, dabbing her mouth with a cloth napkin. "From the sound of it, Star won't have any free time for studying today anyway."

"Thanks, Mags," Mike said, shooting the tutor a grateful smile. "Now Star, here's what you're going to say . . ."

☆ ☆ ☆ ☆ ☆

"Wow," Star whispered to Lola, peeking out through the curtain that blocked off most of the stage of the hotel's ballroom. Just in front of the curtain was a long table with three chairs behind it and a microphone in front of each chair. Beyond that were dozens of men and women holding cameras, tape recorders, and portable computers. "There are more people out there than I expected. Those reporters can't all be from Edinburgh, can they?"

Lola leaned over to take a look. "Doubt it. I guess this whole story is major news," she said quietly. "And I guess I'm mostly to blame for that . . . me and my big mouth!"

"Stop it, Lola," Star said with a smile. "Even Mike says all you did was add fat to the fire. The only one who's really to blame is that reporter back in London who misquoted me in the first place."

Lola shrugged. "I don't know about that," she said. "Stan Starkey probably deserves some of the blame, too." She shook her head, making her long beaded earrings dance. "I swear, that man could turn a hangnail into a front-page story if he thought it would sell more records."

Star giggled. At that moment she felt a hand on her shoulder. Glancing around, she saw Mike looking down at her.

"Ready to go, sweetheart?" he murmured.

"Ready as I'll ever be." Star took a deep breath, trying to calm her fluttering nerves. She didn't really mind doing press conferences, but they weren't her favourite thing in the world, either. Somehow, talking to a couple dozen reporters was much more nerve-wracking than singing to a couple thousand fans.

"Okay," Mike said quietly. "Here's how this will work. We all head out and sit down. I'll go first, say a few words of introduction. Then Lola gives her little speech to apologize for her comments yesterday. When she finishes, I'll nod to you, and you go. Just like we rehearsed."

Star nodded. Mike had gone over the same instructions at least five times since they'd come downstairs – that was how she could tell that he was nervous, too. "Got it," she said, trying to sound confident.

A moment later the three of them were stepping through the curtain onto the stage. There was a sudden buzz of murmuring voices and a whirr of lenses as flashbulbs went off all over the crowded room. Tank and the rest of Star's security team were positioned around the room, along with a few other men Star guessed were from hotel security.

Mike sat down in the centre chair at the table. Star took the seat to his right, perching on the edge of it and resting her elbows on the table. She was careful to keep her expression neutral but pleasant as she looked over at her manager, waiting for him to start. She had carefully pushed all her worries about Dudley – not to mention that stupid dream – out of her mind for the moment, knowing that she had to concentrate on the task at hand.

"Good morning," Mike said into the microphone in front of him, holding up his hand for silence. The crowd of reporters quieted down almost immediately, though flash-bulbs continued to pop intermittently as Mike spoke. "I'm glad y'all could come."

Star was still watching him carefully as he scanned the room. She doubted that anyone else saw the expression of slight surprise that crossed his face as he looked over the gathered reporters, but she knew him well enough to spot it.

"I see some of you have come farther than others," Mike went on. "All the way from London and farther afield, even." He nodded towards a couple of the reporters near the front. "But that's good, I suppose. That way we should be able to put this misunderstanding to rest once and for all and get back to touring. As I'm sure you can imagine, this whole hullabaloo has been about as welcome as an outhouse breeze."

There was a ripple of laughter from the reporters. Star allowed herself a slight smile. Mike always had a slight Texas drawl, but she'd noticed that at certain times it got a lot thicker, and his expressions even more colourful than usual.

Mike quickly introduced Lola, who stood up and smoothed the front of her new Scottish wool sweater, which she was wearing with a pair of zebra-print trousers and hot pink stiletto heels. "I don't have much to say," the stylist began, sounding nervous. "Just that I'm very sorry for the comments I made yesterday. I was trying to defend Star here, and I may have gone over the line. I hope Jade and her people will accept my sincere apology."

As Lola sat down Star leaned forward, glancing past Mike to shoot her a smile. Lola looked back and grinned, obviously relieved to be finished.

Mike was already introducing Star. ". . . so without further ado," he finished, "I give you Miss Star Calloway."

There was a smattering of applause from the audience. But most of the reporters just stared up at her, waiting.

Star cleared her throat. "Thanks, Mike," she said, pulling her microphone a little closer. "I'm really glad to have this chance to talk to you guys today. I've been feeling just awful about this whole thing, because . . . Well, why don't I just tell you exactly what happened? You see, I was talking to a reporter back in London . . ." She paused, scanning the crowd. "I don't think she's here today. But anyway, we were talking at a party, and it was awfully loud, and I'm afraid she might have misheard what I said. Or maybe I just didn't say it very well." She paused just long enough for a shrug and a self-deprecating smile. "See, I was actually trying to compliment Jade – I think she's an amazing talent. And I actually got the opportunity to meet her later that same night, and she's an awesome person, too, one I would be honoured to call a friend. So I certainly never meant to say anything bad about her. I want to join Lola in apologizing, totally and completely, for any hurt feelings that quote might have caused Jade or her team. I just hope I'll get a chance to tell her so in person really soon."

She glanced over at Mike, who nodded and winked,

looking pleased. Out beyond the stage several of the reporters were busy scribbling notes, while others continued to hold up their microphones.

"All right then," Mike said into his own microphone. "There you have it – straight from the horse's mouth, so to speak. Now, I think we have time for a few questions if you—"

Before he could finish the sentence, the entire crowd of reporters seemed to leap forward, all of them shouting at once. The din was so sudden and loud that Star pushed her chair back a few inches, startled. The question-and-answer part of press conferences always seemed to get a little raucous, but she'd never seen anything like this.

"Hold it! Hold it!" Mike was shouting, standing up and waving his arms. "What's wrong with you people? Pipe down, or we're out of here right now!"

His threat seemed to work, and the reporters fell silent again. Star realized she'd been holding her breath and let it out, relieved.

"Now then," Mike continued, still standing. "We'll be takin' your questions one at a time, and no interrupting, please. Okay, Colin – what have you got?"

He pointed to a stylishly dressed man in the front row. Star vaguely recognized the man; he was a British television reporter who'd interviewed her right after her first concert in London.

"Thank you, Mike," the reporter said smoothly. He turned and stared directly at Star. "Star, just before coming in here, we all heard the latest wires out of London bring us the incredible story about your parents' disappearance two years ago. Would you care to comment on that?"

Six

Star was so shocked that she was actually speechless. Her mouth opened and then closed again as she desperately wondered whether she was hallucinating. That reporter hadn't really just asked her about her parents, had he? But that would mean . . .

"All right, this press conference is over!" Mike declared, grasping Star's arm and guiding her behind the curtain. Lola followed a second later, looking just as stunned as the others.

There was a roar of outrage from the reporters, along with more shouted questions. But Star hardly heard any of it. Her mind was reeling.

"Mike," she said blankly. "Did he just . . . ?"

"Afraid so, darlin'," Mike said grimly. "Don't know how it happened, but the story must've broken while we were setting up for the press conference. Blasted bad luck for us."

Lola was staring from one of them to the other, looking

confused. "What was that all about?" she asked. "What was that guy saying about Star's parents, and why is everyone freaking out?"

Star gulped. Before she could say anything, Mike gestured for them to follow him towards the back exit. "Come on," he said. "We can talk about this back upstairs. Let's get out of here while the going's good."

By the time Star, Mike, Lola, Tank, and Mags were gathered around the dining table in their hotel suite, Star's brain was starting to function again. For a few minutes she'd been so stunned that her secret was out that her whole head felt like it was filled with molasses.

"All right, everyone," Mike said as he sat down. "I've just filled Lola in on what's happening, and the rest of you know the story already. What we don't know is how the news leaked out." Just then his cell phone, which was lying on the table at his elbow, rang shrilly. "Excuse me."

Star glanced over at Lola, who looked a little stunned, and made a mental note to apologize to her later for not sharing her secret. Then her mind wandered as Mike spoke briefly with whoever was on the other end of the line – one of their publicists, by the sound of it. She knew that none of the people sitting at the table with her would ever give away her secret. That meant there was only one explanation for what had just happened . . .

Or maybe not, she thought desperately. *Maybe a reporter started sniffing around the Florida police files and made a connection. Or maybe someone back home in New Limpet blabbed – maybe even Nans. She doesn't always remember that she shouldn't talk to reporters as if they're just neighbours from down the block.*

But as Mike hung up from his call, Star couldn't hold her thoughts in any longer. "I'm sorry," she blurted out. "This is all my fault!"

The adults turned to stare at her. "Your fault?" Mike said in surprise. "What are you talkin' about, Star?"

Star took a deep breath. "I didn't mention it before because it didn't seem important," she said. "But remember back in London, when I was talking to Jade in the bathroom? Well, we were, like, sharing secrets and stuff, and I sort of told her about my family."

"Sort of?" Mags cocked an eyebrow at her.

Star smiled weakly. "Okay, not sort of," she said, feeling

tears welling up in her eyes. "Totally. I totally blabbed the whole story. I – I thought I could trust her. She didn't seem like the type of person who . . ." She gulped, letting her voice trail off before her tears spilled over.

She expected Mike to get angry, maybe remind her of how many times he'd warned her against letting the press get wind of her secret. Instead he merely sighed and rubbed his forehead.

"It's all right, little one," he told Star. "It had to come out sooner or later. I was just hopin' it would be, you know, *later*."

Mags nodded thoughtfully. "We all knew we couldn't keep this a secret forever," she told Star. "We knew the truth would come out at some point. Still, it's a bit of a shock now that it's actually happened."

"And we know it's been tough on you, *chica*," Tank added, smiling at Star. "That's an important part of your life, and you've kept it a secret this long while living right smack in the public eye. Very impressive, really – most adults couldn't pull it off, let alone someone your age."

Somehow, the fact that they were all being so understanding made Star feel even worse. "I'm sorry I let you down," she whispered. "I really didn't think she'd say anything."

Mike shook his head. "Not your fault," he said gruffly. "If anyone's to blame, it's me. It was my idea to keep the secret in the first place – maybe that wasn't too bright."

"Stop it," Mags told him sternly. "You can go ahead and beat yourself up later – right now we've got a situation to deal with."

Mike glanced at her and nodded. "You're right," he said. "It really doesn't matter if Jade was the one who blabbed, or more likely, that old cuss Starkey – this sort of trick would be right up his alley. However the cat got out of the bag, we've got to deal with the results. Now, here's what I suggest . . ."

The four adults started discussing strategies for dealing with the press and the public, but Star's mind was drifting again. She still couldn't quite believe that Jade had ratted her out.

She just didn't seem like that kind of girl, she thought, once again recalling her conversation with Jade. *Did I misjudge her that much? I mean, Lola is always telling me I only see the best in people . . .*

She could still see the vulnerable look on Jade's face when

she'd admitted to hating her own hit song. Even though Jade's secret wasn't nearly as juicy as her own, Star had given her word to keep it. That meant she would never in a million years share it with anyone, except maybe Missy — after all, that was what best friends were for.

But I'll never breathe a word about it to anyone else, not even Mike, Star thought. *How could Jade do this?*

She tuned back in to the conversation at the table just in time to hear Mike sigh again. "Look, no matter how we go about it, there's really not much we can do here," he said wearily. "After all, the story is true."

"Right," Mags said matter-of-factly. "Maybe it's better that it's out in the open. Now we can stop watching what we say."

Mike didn't look entirely convinced, but he nodded. "True."

Star's hand crept up to touch her star necklace as she thought about what Mags had just said. Maybe it was all for the best. Wasn't she always thinking how much easier it would be if she didn't have to hide so much about herself?

She glanced at Lola, who hadn't said much and still looked somewhat dazed and confused. Now she wouldn't have to be kept in the dark. Now Star wouldn't have to sidestep around interviewers' questions about her past. Now Missy and Nans and her other friends back home wouldn't have to be always on guard against reporters asking tricky questions.

Best of all, Star added to herself, *now that more people know that my parents and Timmy are missing, they'll be found sooner! I always thought it would help to have the whole world helping me look for them.*

She brightened at the thought, though she almost immediately felt guilty about it. Mike had put so much effort into protecting her secret for the past two years . . . Still, now that she was getting used to the idea that it was suddenly out in the open, she couldn't help admitting that it was sort of a relief.

Who knows? she thought, her natural optimism taking over at last. *Maybe I'll actually end up thanking Jade for this in the end.*

"Well, you were right," Mike told Star a few hours later as he hurried back into the suite. He had been out meeting with publicists and others all afternoon. "Jade was the one who blabbed. Seems there was a big exclusive about it on the BBC news. That's where the wire services picked it up."

Star nodded, not at all surprised. She was sitting on the floor of the suite's main room trying to get Dudley to sit on her lap. The vet Mags had hired had come and gone, reporting that Dudley was in perfect physical health.

"Maybe he needs psychological help," she mused aloud as the little dog wriggled out of her grip once again. "Dogs can probably have mental problems just like people, right?"

"Huh?" Mike said blankly. "What's that?"

"Never mind."

Star sighed, realizing that she was probably the only person around who wasn't completely focused on her own past. If she'd thought her little nonrivalry with Jade was big news, this new story was *huge*.

"Like Godzilla's older brother," she murmured. "On steroids."

"Huh?" Mike looked at her worriedly. "Don't wig out on me now, darlin' – we all need to stay focused until this thing blows over."

"Sorry," Star said. "I know. And I'm fine." She shrugged. "I just can't believe everyone is so . . . so *interested* in this."

She gestured at the TV, which was muted. It was tuned

to PopTV, the all-music station. A video had just ended, and a dark-haired female VJ was talking in front of a picture of Star.

"Turn it up," Mike said.

Star leaned over, grabbed the remote from the coffee table, and hit the volume button. The VJ's bright, perky voice filled the room.

". . . Florida police could not be reached for comment," the VJ was saying. "But we've just heard from a reliable source that Star has hired a full-time psychic to travel with her and channel messages from her lost parents. We'll have more details as soon as we get them. In the meantime this is Lucita for PopTV, now returning you to your regular programming. Stay tuned for more Star updates as additional news comes in."

Star couldn't believe what she'd just heard. "That's not true!" she exclaimed. "The part about the psychic, I mean."

"I know that, sweetheart." Mike shook his head sadly. "Better prepare yourself – you're going to feel like a gnat in a hailstorm for a while, I reckon, and a lot of people aren't going to stop and wonder what's the truth and what isn't. Not that this story isn't juicy enough without all the extra toppings." He glanced at her. "That reminds me, did you reach your grandmother yet? I'm sure it'll be all over the evening news back in the U.S. within a couple of hours. And it's only a matter of time before the vultures track her down for an interview, if they haven't already."

Star climbed to her feet. "I'll go try to reach her again right now."

Things only got crazier as the day wore on. By dinnertime PopTV was running updates on the half hour, while most of the major news agencies already had teams camped out in New Limpet as well as in Edinburgh. All of the British tabloids had Star splashed across their front pages with headlines like STAR'S SIZZLING SECRET!, while more respectable newspapers from all over the world were only slightly more subdued in their coverage. Most of the major weekly news magazines from around the world had called asking for interviews, and the biggest Web site devoted to Star, named *Star Power* after her first album, had received so many e-mails that it had crashed. It was all even more overwhelming than the media attention Star had received when her first single reached number one, though not in such a positive way. Star was used to being in the limelight, but all the sudden extra attention made her feel a little like a fly trapped between two panes in a window – helpless and totally exposed.

Trying to avoid the reporters, who were gathering around the hotel like pilgrims around a religious shrine, she had stayed in the hotel suite all day worrying about Dudley, who was still acting strange, and trying to focus on the book about Hadrian's Wall, which she still hadn't finished. She'd also spoken to Nans on the phone, explaining the situation. Then she'd tried to call Missy, but there had been no answer at her house and she'd had to do her best to explain what was going on to the Takamoris' answering machine.

As evening fell she finally gave up on the Hadrian's Wall book completely and was pacing near the door waiting for room service to arrive. "How long ago did we order?" she asked Tank and Lola, who were the only other people in the suite. Mags had gone out to run some errands, and Mike was meeting with the publicists again.

Lola checked her watch, then shrugged. "I don't remember," she said. "It's been a while."

"The kitchen's probably having to wait for their food deliveries to swim through that sea of humanity camped outside the hotel," Tank put in from the couch near the window, where he was reading a thick Russian novel. "I believe this is the first time we've had to wait more than twenty minutes for—"

A loud rap on the door interrupted him. "A-ha!" Star cried happily. "Chuck wagon's pullin' in," she added in a pretty good imitation of Mike's Texas drawl.

She hurried to the door and opened it wide. In the hallway was a cart laden with food. A young bearded man wearing an apron stood behind it.

"I'll bring it inside, shall I?" the man said in a British accent.

Star stepped back to let him pass. "Thanks," she said as he wheeled the cart into the room. He stopped just inside and stared around blankly.

"Right over there," Lola said, pointing to the table.

"Of course, of course," the man said hastily, shoving the cart so hard in that direction that a pitcher of water tipped over, splashing its contents all over the covered silver food trays. "Oops, so sorry – let me just grab something to clean that up."

He reached under the cart to the lowest shelf. But instead of pulling out a cloth or sponge, his hand emerged clutching a camera.

"Smile!" he crowed, immediately snapping several pictures of Star.

Star was so shocked that she couldn't move. Luckily Tank wasn't similarly affected. He leaped off the couch instantly, dropping his book as he dived across the room and grabbed the man.

"Nice try, buddy," he barked, pinning the fake waiter's arms behind his back and wrestling him towards the door. "Lola, get the film," he added over his shoulder, raising his voice to be heard over Dudley's barks as the little dog raced in from the bedroom.

Star grabbed Dudley to keep him out of the way and then watched, still feeling stunned, as Lola caught the camera Tank tossed her. She fiddled with the back of it. "Drat," she muttered. "I can never figure out how these things – oops! There it is," she interrupted herself as the back of the camera suddenly popped open. She yanked out the half-exposed film and stuck it in the pocket of her baggy leopard-print trousers before handing the camera back to

Tank, who had the intruder halfway out the door by then.

"Oi! Give me that film!" the man shouted at Lola. "It's my personal property; I'll have you arrested for theft!"

"You go ahead and do that," Tank growled. He glanced over his shoulder at Lola and Star. "Lock the door behind me," he told them. "I'll be back after I drop this *payaso* off with hotel security."

Lola hurried forward as Tank shoved the intruder into the hall. She closed and bolted the door behind them, then collapsed against it.

"Whew!" she said. "That was crazy, huh? Some of those reporters will do anything for a story." She straightened up and wandered over to the cart, peeking under a couple of the covered plates. "Hey, at least it looks like this is our real dinner order. Come on, babydoll, let's help ourselves to the fries before Tank gets back – you know how he likes to hog them."

Star smiled weakly and headed for the table, not wanting to admit that she'd totally lost her appetite.

Seven

"Good morning, everyone, this is Bonny Donny Mackin coming to you live from right here in Edinburgh," the DJ said into his microphone in a lilting Scottish brogue. "I'm lucky enough to be sitting here with Star Calloway, the American pop star who will be playing tonight the first of her two concerts here in town." The DJ winked at Star through the glass of the tiny recording booth. "And it's bound to be a fair barry show, since the whole hoachin' world seems to be watching Star at the moment. Welcome, Star."

Star smiled weakly, wondering if it had been a mistake to insist on rescheduling this interview, which had been postponed after the uproar the day before. "Hello, Donny. And hello out there, everyone listening," she said, adjusting the earphones on her head as she spoke into the microphone on the desk in front of her. "It's nice to be here in beautiful Edinburgh."

"Aye," Donny replied. "Now, Star, you know I have to ask – what's all this business about yer parents and all that? Is what I've been reading in the papers true?"

Star took a deep breath. Mike had warned her that the interviewer would want to talk about this, and had coached her on what to say. Somehow, though, she couldn't help being surprised that the DJ hadn't started off with at least a few questions about her new album or that night's concert.

"Most of it's true, Donny," she said, carefully sticking to the responses Mike had taught her. "Of course, some of the reporters are going a little overboard. But it's true that my parents and brother went missing two years ago, and that their disappearance remains officially unsolved."

"I see, I see – how interesting," Donny said. "But it must be hard on you, not knowing what's happened to them, then, aye?"

Star reached up and touched her star necklace, wishing she could answer honestly. But once again she forced herself to stick to the script. "It's difficult, yes," she said blandly. "But I keep pretty busy, especially now with this tour, so that helps keep my mind off of things a little."

The DJ leaned forward in his booth, peering at her

curiously through the glass. "Och, but you must be always wondering what's become of them," he said. "What d'ye think, Star? Are they out there somewhere, or gone forever?"

Star winced at the blunt question, then glanced over her shoulder at the studio door, half expecting Mike to burst in and end the interview. "There's no way of knowing that, of course," she said, glad that Mike had prepared her for this question, too, even though she had insisted that no one would be bold enough to ask. "But I remain hopeful."

"All right then," Donny said cheerfully. "We have to hear a word from our sponsors now, but we'll be back shortly to talk more with Star Calloway."

As the DJ punched a button to start the commercials, Star slumped in her seat, relieved for the break. She realized she was still clutching her star necklace in one slightly trembling hand.

Glancing at the studio window, she saw Mike peering in at her through the small glass window in the door. He gave her a thumbs-up, and she smiled.

I can handle this, she thought. *I know I can. Mike and the others have faith in me. I can't let them down – or my fans, either. Besides, Mom and Dad didn't raise me to be a quitter.*

Sitting up a little straighter, Star adjusted her headphones and waited for her next cue.

Star stepped out of the radio station building half an hour later, flanked by Mike and Tank, to find that the sun had broken through the clouds while she was inside. It was turning into a gorgeous summer day, though the temperature still couldn't be much above sixty-five degrees, and Star was glad to be wearing the stylish but warm cotton jacket Lola had helped her pick out that morning.

"Wow," she said. "I was starting to forget what the sun looks like!"

Mike and Tank chuckled. Before they could answer, the sound of excited shouting reached them.

Turning, Star saw at least a dozen reporters and cameramen racing across the parking area towards them, dodging or leaping over the parked cars. "Uh-oh," she said softly.

"Let's go," Tank snapped, grabbing Star by her right arm as Mike took her left one. "Come on, to the limo, *pronto*!"

Star's heart pounded as she ran, half-lifted off her feet a few times by the two men. The limo was just ahead, and

Tank was already holding the automatic lock clicker in his free hand.

As Mike ripped open the back door, Star glanced over her shoulder. The fastest of the reporters was only about ten yards away. For a second she froze, startled and a little scared by the hungry, almost menacing gleam in his eye.

"Star!" the reporter shouted when he saw her looking, his straight, limp blonde hair flopping as he ran. "Will you give us a statement? Did the police find any evidence of a boating accident, or do you suspect foul play?"

Another reporter, a pinched-looking woman in a bright red dress, was right behind him. "Do you believe in reincarnation, Star?" she screeched. "Will you someday name your children after your lost parents?"

Suddenly Mike pulled Star forward into the car and leaped in after her. Tank was already in the driver's seat.

As Mike and Star collapsed onto the padded leather seats, Tank quickly hit a button on the car's console. There was a satisfying *thunk* as the doors locked once again.

The first of the pursuers reached the limo a second later and pounded on it in frustration. The sound was muffled by the car's solid body and extra-thick windows.

"That was close," Tank said, breathing heavily as he started the engine. "From now on, we'd better make sure we have reinforcements whenever we leave the hotel."

Mike nodded. "My mistake," he said heavily. "Figured this early, we'd be able to sneak out the back." He glanced at Star. "Sorry you had to go through that, kiddo. Are you okay?"

Star nodded but didn't say anything. She was still too shaken up by what had just happened. *I guess this is what Mike was trying to protect me from all these years,* she thought shakily, trying to forget the reporters' disturbing questions. *No wonder . . .*

"Settle down, Dudley," Star said sternly. "Otherwise you can't take a nap with me at all."

She held the little dog firmly on the bed beside her until he stopped squirming. Then she pulled up the covers, draping them over Dudley's shoulders as well as her own.

Closing her eyes, she yawned and snuggled up against the dog's warm little body. It was just after lunchtime, but she was already exhausted. She'd had to get up early for the radio interview, and she hadn't slept well the night before – partly because she was worried about what was going on, and partly because Dudley had refused to stay still for more than fifteen minutes at a time all night. When Mags had noticed her drooping eyelids at lunch, she insisted that Star take a nap as soon as she finished eating. Mike had seconded the idea, reminding her that she had a concert that night.

For once, the thought of performing failed to fill Star with any hint of excitement or enthusiasm. Instead she felt only weariness.

I've got to get some rest, and then get psyched up for tonight, she thought as sleep drifted over her like a shadow dimming her mind. *I've got to forget about everything else and focus on the show.*

The next thing she knew, she was trapped in a close, damp, clinging place, the sound of rushing water all around her. The only thing she could see was something white, smooth, and gleaming in the dim light. Panic overcame her as she struggled towards the object, knowing that it was important but not quite sure why. She reached towards it, but no matter how she stretched, it stayed just out of reach.

She awoke a second later with a start, sitting up in bed so

fast that Dudley almost tumbled off onto the floor. The little dog whined in protest, scrabbling back beneath the sheets.

"I know what it was, Dudley!" Star gasped, swiping at a clump of hair clinging damply to her forehead. "That white thing I saw last time – it was a bone! A bleached bone, somewhere with a lot of water . . ."

She grimaced as an image popped into her head: white-caps crashing onto a beach, the swell and retreat of the water steady and relentless. She knew that beach – thanks to all the recent talk about her parents, it had been in her mind all the time lately.

The rushing water sound from her dream filled her mind, bringing with it all sorts of uncomfortable thoughts – the beach, the ocean, that boat ride . . . and bone. That bleached white glint of bone . . .

Star shuddered, banishing the whole line of thought before it could go any further. She was giving herself the creeps, and she didn't want to think too hard about why she was having such weird dreams all of a sudden.

"It's nothing," she whispered, grabbing Dudley and nearly smothering him in a big hug. "I'm just overtired, that's all. Everybody knows dreams don't mean anything."

☆ ☆ ☆ ☆ ☆

"Are you sure there's no way those reporters can get in and mess things up?" Star asked anxiously, raising her arms above her head as Lola made some last-minute adjustments to her stage outfit.

"Sure as a dog has fleas," Mike said calmly. "This show's been sold out since long before the news broke, and the freelancers won't be able to get in without tickets. Plus we're keeping a tight rein on the personnel who're here covering the show from the local radio stations and what-not. Nobody's going to make any trouble if we can help it."

Star nodded. She knew that Mike and Tank and the rest of the team were doing all they could to minimize the effects of the media frenzy that was still going on outside. Now that it was almost time to go onstage for her first Edinburgh concert, some of her usual preperformance excitement was creeping back. But it was muted by everything that had happened over the past two days.

"Arms down," Lola said, stepping back and casting a critical eye over Star. "Okay, I think you're all set. You look perfect!"

"Thanks." Star smiled at Lola and then glanced at herself in the full-length mirror on the dressing room wall. She looked about the same as she always did before a show – dressed in one of Lola's custom-designed outfits, her hair and stage make-up looking great, her bright blue eyes sparkling.

Mike handed over her headset and Star put it on, blowing into the tiny microphone to make sure it was working. Then she followed Mike out of the dressing room and into the long hall leading to the backstage area. Security guards were posted every twenty yards or so all the way down the hall.

"Just in case," Mike murmured when he noticed Star staring at them.

She nodded wordlessly. Mike led the way to a plain grey door. He put his hand on the knob and then glanced down at her.

"Ready?" he asked.

"Ready," Star said. She was a little surprised by how normal her voice sounded.

Mike opened the door, releasing a solid wall of sound. But this was very different from the howls of the reporters outside, with their rude shouted questions. This was a sound Star lived for – the cheers and whistles of thousands of excited fans who couldn't wait to see their idol live onstage.

Suddenly it was as if all the tension of the past two days whooshed out of her and trickled away like water squeezed out of a sponge. Feeling real excitement burning inside of her at last, Star blew a kiss in Mike's direction, then ran lightly up the steps across the backstage area. She peeked out front just long enough to make sure that the band and dancers were in place. Then she took a deep breath and leaped out onto the stage.

"Hi there, Edinburgh!" she yelled, though her voice was hardly audible as the crowd's wild roars swelled to double volume at her appearance. "It's great to be here!"

She just stood there for a moment, soaking in the heady, familiar feeling. The crowd of rabid reporters that was probably waiting for her outside flickered briefly through her mind, but she pushed the thought away.

This is why I'm here, she reminded herself, squinting past the bright lights at the fans who were screaming, yelling, waving their handmade signs or the brand-new Star Calloway T-shirts they'd just bought, and jumping up and down with joy at being there. *No matter what the latest gossip is in the tabloids, these fans are here to have a good time. And I'm going to make sure they get what they came for.*

With that, she raised her arm to signal the band to start. As the familiar chords of her opening song poured out of the amplifiers, she prepared to throw herself into the performance just like always.

Eight

The ebullient mood she'd captured at the concert lingered with Star through the night, chasing away most of her remaining uneasy thoughts and easing her into a deep, restful, dreamless sleep. The next morning she woke up late, still feeling pumped up and happy. Sunlight – only slightly muted by the usual grey clouds – poured through the bedroom windows. Star smiled and sat up in bed to stretch, realizing that she was already looking forward to the second Edinburgh show the following evening.

Dudley was nowhere in sight, but she could hear the faint buzz of voices from elsewhere in the hotel suite. Leaping out of bed, she hurried out to the main room in her pyjamas and robe to find Mike, Mags, and Tank gathered there sipping coffee and staring at the TV.

"Morning," she said with a yawn. "What's for breakfast? I'm starved."

"Hush a sec, darlin'," Mike said, gesturing towards the TV

screen. "You're just in time. Jade's supposed to make some kind of statement to the press – they just broke into the countdown for it."

"Oh!" In all the hubbub over her parents, Star had almost forgotten about Jade. Remembering how the whole mess had started, she felt a little of her happy mood slip away. She sank onto the arm of the couch where the others were sitting and stared at the TV.

On the screen one of the PopTV VJs was just winding up a summary of Jade's career. "As most pop music fans know by now," the VJ continued, "Jade was recently in the news because of some remarks that fellow American pop idol Star Calloway made to a London reporter. We now take you live to the Londonia Hotel, where Jade has just stepped out to make a statement about that."

The picture cut away to show Jade standing in front of the luxurious London hotel's gold-bordered glass doors. Stan Starkey was right behind her, and several beefy bodyguards surrounded the two of them. In the background Star thought she caught a glimpse of Stan's assistant, Manda Smith.

"Good morning," Jade said coolly to the cameras, glancing down at a sheet of paper she was holding. "I'm here to address a few things that have been going on lately. First of all, I want to say that I've only met Star Calloway once for like, five minutes. She and I are *not* friends, we've never *been* friends, and I'm really not interested in *being* friends after all that's happened. I'd like to go on record as saying that I believe we all have to take responsibility for the things we say and do, and that we should consider how our words might affect others before we say them. However, despite my lack of respect for Star's immature comments that started all this, I'm going to accept her apology and move on. I suggest that she do the same so we can both put this ridiculous situation behind us. Thank you, that's all I have to say."

Star felt as if she'd just been slugged in the gut. "Wow," she said as Jade disappeared into the hotel with her team and the TV picture shifted back to the VJ. "That was pretty harsh."

She couldn't help feeling hurt by what Jade had said. Where was the reserved yet cautiously friendly girl she'd met in the ladies' room just a few days earlier? That Jade had seemed smart and understanding, like someone who might make a good friend once they knew each other a little better. The Jade she'd just seen on TV seemed like a completely different person.

Mike set down his coffee cup. "Try not to take it personally, Star," he said kindly. "Starkey's behind this – you can count on it. With all the business about your folks' disappearance dominating the airwaves lately, he's just trying to get back in the game. It's like that business with Eddie Urbane before we left. He didn't try to mess up your tour because of anything you did, or even because he doesn't like you. It was just him trying to get ahead any way he could. And that's what Miss Jade is up to, too, you can count on it."

"I guess." Star realized that Mike's words made sense. But did that excuse Jade's comments? "I just wasn't expecting something like this from her."

She looked around, expecting Lola's usual comment: *That's because you always expect the best of people, Star.* Then she realized that the stylist wasn't in the room.

"Where's Lola?" she asked.

"Errands," Tank replied. "She slipped out before any of us woke up this morning."

Mike looked a little sour. "Right," he said. "Guess she wasn't listenin' when I said we should stick tight around the campfire here except in an emergency."

"Look," Mags blurted, pointing to the television. "Star's on again."

Star turned to see a picture of herself onscreen behind the VJ. "What are they saying now?" she asked wearily. Mags reached for the remote and turned up the volume. The VJ was summarizing Star's family situation yet again.

"And now," the VJ said brightly, "we take you to Star's hometown of New Limpet, Pennsylvania, for a live update."

Star groaned, caught between dismay and homesickness as the picture flashed to a shot of the New Limpet town sign. "They're really there," she murmured.

She recognized the scruffily cute, young PopTV VJ who was doing the live report. "Hey kids, Bash here, just chiz-zil-in' in New Limpet, P.A.," he said, leaning one elbow on the top of the town sign and grinning lazily into the camera. "This is it – the scene of the crime, the site of the sizzle. It's about five p.m. here, and reporters are swarming in from all over, but they're not having an easy time – seems Star's homies are used to keeping her past on the down-low. To see what I mean, check out this footage from earlier today."

The picture shifted again. First it showed an exterior view of Nans's house. Then it cut away to the middle school Star had attended before becoming famous. Finally it settled on a different PopTV reporter standing on the sidewalk near the school. A moment later several kids Star's age emerged and started walking away. The reporter followed them.

"Anyone here know Star Calloway?" the reporter called.

One of the kids, a boy with wavy brown hair, glanced over his shoulder with an anxious expression on his face. "Leave us alone," he called out.

Star gasped. "Aaron!" she shrieked. "That's Aaron Bickford!"

As soon as the words left her mouth, she blushed. Aaron was the closest thing she'd ever had to a boyfriend. The two of them had just started looking at each other as more than friends when her sudden rise to superstardom exploded. Just before she'd left on the tour, he'd sort of, kind of, finally almost admitted to liking her – they'd even almost kissed! She couldn't believe she was watching him on TV, running down the sidewalk with his friends to escape from the reporter.

She moaned and leaned back against Mike's shoulder as the picture changed again, this time showing one of Nans's neighbors. "I can't believe they're doing this," she exclaimed. "I can't believe they're hounding my friends and family – all because of me."

"Maybe it's time to change the channel," Tank suggested, reaching for the remote. He flipped through several channels, then stopped. "Uh-oh. Here's another one."

Star looked up and saw her own face again. This time the logo in the bottom corner of the screen read CNC, for the Celebrity News Channel.

". . . be sure to tune in tonight for a special edition of *Between the Notes,* featuring Star Calloway," the polished blonde female reporter was saying from behind the Celebrity News anchor desk. "The show tells the whole story of Star's rise to fame and fortune. And we're updating it as we speak to include all the latest information out of London, Florida, and Pennsylvania."

Tank changed channels again, finally settling on Weather24-7, the all-weather station. "This should be safe," he joked weakly.

Star sighed. "It's okay, Tank. I don't mind watching the

other stuff. It's probably better if we know what everyone is saying."

After a while the adults wandered off to take care of other business, but Star spent another hour sitting in front of the TV flipping from channel to channel. She was shocked at how quickly the media were digging up information about her family. Reporters had already interviewed most of her old neighbours, found ancient yearbook pictures of her parents, even tracked down a nurse at the hospital where her little brother was born. And the more information they found, the more eager they seemed to find more.

Star shook her head, caught between amusement and dismay as she watched a well-known news anchor specu-late about whether the Calloways could have entered the Witness Protection Programme without telling their daughter. It was overwhelming seeing her life dissected in front of the world – and more than a little weird, too. To Star herself, her family's disappearance was still the most important news ever. But she couldn't help thinking that it was sort of bizarre to see it splashed all over the TV and newspapers as if that two-year-old mystery were the only thing worth talking about in the entire world. She knew there were wars going on right at that moment, important elections taking place in different countries, and unemployment and famine and all sorts of other serious events happening all over. But because Star was a celebrity, everyone was acting like her story was the biggest thing going. Accomplished reporters were spending their time sniffing out old yearbook pictures of her parents and chasing Aaron Bickford down the street like he was a celebrity himself. It didn't make much sense when she really thought about it, and yet she realized it was the kind of thing that happened all the time – except this time it was happening to her.

Star was watching yet another special report about herself a few minutes later when the suite's main door swung open and Lola hurried in, wearing a bright red rain hat with her favourite purple-and-gold shawl and an emerald green dress. She was carrying a shopping bag.

"I'm back," she called out breathlessly.

Mike, who was working on a press release at the dining table, looked up. "What's the matter?"

Noticing the sharp tone in Mike's voice, Star looked over at Lola as well. The stylist had a sheepish look on her face.

"What do you mean?" Lola began, then gave up and collapsed on the nearest chair. "Oh, all right, you caught me. I might have – er – said a little something to the reporters outside. Something that, well, might not be exactly true. So to speak."

"Aargh!" Mike put his hands to his head. "Lola, we've talked about this . . . What did you say?"

"Um, remember that business about the psychic?" Lola asked. "You know, that story they were reporting on PopTV? Well, one of the vultures outside yelled some question about that – for some reason, they seemed to think *I* might be Star's psychic."

Star looked from Lola's long fringed shawl to her usual armful of bangle bracelets and smiled. But Mike didn't look amused. "And?" he prompted sternly.

"And I told them I wasn't a psychic," Lola said. "But, um, then I said I'd just heard that Madame Stupenda – you know, that super-famous TV psychic out in Hollywood? – that she'd just foreseen that Star's family would turn up safe and sound sometime in the next six months." Lola glanced contritely at Star. "Sorry, babydoll. I know it's wrong to lie. I just couldn't stand some of the rude questions they were asking."

"It's okay." Star smiled at her reassuringly. "It's not like they need your help to make stuff up anyway."

Mike just groaned, rubbed his head, and started muttering something that sounded suspiciously like his own prediction about how much worse the media circus was going to get. Meanwhile Star noticed Dudley trotting purposefully into the room. Realizing she hadn't seen him all morning, she whistled for him to come to her.

Ignoring the whistle, Dudley continued on his way, heading straight for his dog bed, which was sitting on the floor near the TV. Star brought the soft fabric bed with her everywhere they went, though the little dog rarely slept on it, preferring the end of Star's bed.

As she watched, Dudley leaped onto his bed, scrabbling furiously at the fabric as if digging for moles in a garden.

"Hey," Star said. "Dudley, stop that! You're going to rip it."

Jumping to her feet, she hurried over and grabbed the little dog, lifting him away from the bed. Dudley whined and squirmed, trying to get free.

"Ouch," she said as one of his hind claws caught her on the arm. "Quit it, Dudley! You're acting like a nut!"

She set him down and twisted her arm around, looking

to see if the scratch was bleeding. Dudley immediately returned to digging in his bed. Star reached down and grabbed the edge of the dog bed, dumping Dudley onto the floor. Tossing the bed on top of the TV cabinet, she stared at her dog worriedly. The vet had said there was nothing wrong with him. But if that was true, why was he acting so strange?

Nine

"No!" Star cried, wrestling with her covers.

For a second she couldn't remember where she was. The room was dark, chilly, and slightly damp, and the muffled sounds of an unfamiliar city drifted in through the windows. She felt around for Dudley, but his warm, pudgy body was nowhere to be found.

Star forced herself to lean back against her pillow, which was damp with sweat despite the cool temperature. She'd been having that dream again. The rushing water sounds, the glint of bleached bone, and the suffocating feeling of hopelessness were all imprinted in her mind.

Okay, this is getting really stupid, Star told herself, taking a deep breath and trying to calm her racing heart.

She shuddered, unable to shake the creepy feeling the dream had left her with. Wiping her clammy hands on her pyjamas, she tried to do as Mags would probably suggest and look at the situation logically. Her life was even crazier than usual at the moment – wasn't that reason enough to be feeling a little off-kilter even while asleep?

Or maybe that isn't it at all, Star thought, pulling the sheets up to her chin and staring at the darkened ceiling. *Maybe my dreams are trying to tell me something. Maybe they mean something – sort of a sign, or a prediction like from that psychic everybody thinks I hired.*

She bit her lip, not wanting to think about what exactly that might mean. But lying there in the dark – by herself, in a hotel room in a strange city – she couldn't seem to stop her mind from rushing along anyway. A lot of the reporters who'd been hounding her over the past couple of days seemed to think that her parents would never come home. Some even looked at her as if they thought she was a fool to keep her hopes alive. Maybe that was what Mike had really been protecting her from all along – maybe he thought the worst, too.

Are they right? Star thought, hugging the bedclothes to herself and feeling more alone than she'd ever felt in her life. *Are my dreams just trying to tell me what I can't admit when I'm awake?*

Star spent most of the next morning moping around the hotel suite, too distracted to focus on anything. She tried doing her homework, but gave that up after reading the same paragraph in her history book four times. Then she pulled out her hand-held and checked in on Missy again. But Missy's e-mail still seemed to be on the blink, and the only interesting thing in her inbox was a message from Eddie Urbane.

That's weird, she thought. *He's never e-mailed me before. I didn't even know he had my address.* Dully curious, she clicked it open.

From: urbanesmyname

To: singingstar01

Subject: hi star, from eddie urbane!

so sorry 2 hear of yr troubles. do let me know if there's ne-thing I can do.

did u see the cover story in Pop-o-rama magazine this week? I just saw it myself, hot off the presses. I can't believe they called u "a future has-been" — totally unfair 2 kick u when u're down!

E.

Star winced. She hadn't seen the story in question – with everything else that was going on, she hadn't bothered to flip through the daily pile of press clippings in several days. With a sigh she deleted Eddie's message without responding. She wandered around the suite for a few more minutes, trying to figure out a useful way to divert herself from her own thoughts.

Finally she gave up on doing anything productive and flopped on the couch to watch TV. Mike walked in a few minutes later as she was flipping through the channels, hardly pausing on any of them for more than five seconds.

"You all right, darlin'?" he asked, looking concerned.

Star shrugged. "Been better."

"Look, Star," Mike said soothingly. "I know it doesn't seem like it right now, but this crazy media hootenanny will die down after a while. Some other celebrity will get married, or say something controversial, or do something outrageous, and the whole pack of hounds will tear off after them and leave us alone. All we have to do for now is keep our heads down and wait it out. Okay?"

Star could tell that he thought her mood was solely from the pressure of dealing with the media storm that surrounded them. She didn't bother to correct him. The last thing she wanted to do was explain about her dreams and her dark thoughts to anyone – even the people she trusted the most. Talking about it might make it all come true, and she wasn't sure she could handle that.

"Okay," she said to Mike. To her surprise, her voice sounded almost normal. "Thanks. I'm all right. Maybe I'll see if Tank wants to go help me work out for a while."

Mike looked slightly surprised. Though Star spent an hour or so jogging or in the gym on most of her days off to keep in shape for dancing, on concert days she normally liked to save her energy for the performance itself.

"Sorry, sweetheart," he said. "I just sent him out to the embassy to double-check on some visas we'll need when we get over to the Continent. I reckon he'll be back in an hour or two, though."

Star sighed and sank back against the couch. A good workout might have taken her mind off of things. But Mike would never let her go down to the hotel gym alone, even if the staff agreed to close it off to outsiders as usual. It was just too risky.

Instead she resumed her channel surfing as Mike's cell phone rang and he wandered off with it pressed to his ear. Just like the day before, every other channel seemed to be doing some kind of special report on her. Even Weather24-7 had got into the act with a story about riptides and other dangerous weather patterns off the Florida coast.

She was relieved and surprised when she flipped to PopTV and found that they had taken a break from her story. Instead they were airing a rerun of a recent exposé about ticket scalping.

Star had seen part of the show before, but she settled back to watch, happy to see anything that wasn't directly about her. The reporter was in the middle of interviewing a bunch of teenage fans who had been shut out of a recent show by the hot boy band Boysterous. The kids complained that scalpers had bought out a large percentage of the tickets and then resold them at such high prices that many of the band's most loyal fans couldn't afford to go.

Then the focus shifted to the scalpers themselves. One scalper had agreed to be interviewed on camera as long as his face was blurred.

"Hey, I know it's illegal," the man said defiantly. "But what's the big deal? If I get there first with the money, why shouldn't I buy as many tickets as I can? It's called free enterprise, you know. And I'm trying to make a living – I'm not going to sell at a loss just so a bunch of whiny kids can afford to—"

Star clicked off the TV, interrupting the scalper in mid-sentence. Somehow the story was making her more depressed than ever.

Maybe nothing is as good as I think it is, she thought glumly, staring at the blank TV screen. *Maybe all those fans I imagine I'm singing to while I'm up onstage are actually getting locked out of the shows by scalpers. Maybe that nice girl Jade I thought I met really is a coldhearted snake like she seems on TV. And maybe, just maybe, I'm foolish to believe that my parents are out there somewhere waiting for me to find them.*

Star was a wreck by the time she was supposed to go onstage that night. "Are you sure you're going to be okay?" Mike asked worriedly as he held open the dressing room door.

"I'm fine," Star lied. She bent down to hug Dudley for luck as usual. But he wriggled out of her grip with a whine of annoyance. As she straightened up she touched her star necklace, trying to draw on the strength and comfort it had always given her. But for the first time it felt like just a tiny chunk of cold metal in her hand.

She followed Mike towards the stage door, trying desperately to pump herself up for the coming performance. But as she stepped onstage a moment later to the hysterical cheers of the crowd, she felt like the world's biggest fraud.

What am I doing here? she wondered bleakly as the bright stage lights dipped and swirled over the stage, making the entire auditorium look like the view from a roller-coaster ride. Still, she knew she had to get through the show – there were thousands of people out there who had paid good money to be entertained.

"Hello, Edinburgh!" Star shouted in her microphone, pretending to be thrilled and excited. She signalled for the band to start right away, wanting to get the show over with as quickly as possible.

The band sounded great, and her voice poured out of the speakers as strong and pure as ever. But with her usual energy and enthusiasm missing, Star couldn't quite seem to keep up with her own song. She flubbed the lyrics at the beginning of the second verse, and at one point when the backup dancers were going left, she accidentally went right, almost colliding with the dancers in the front row.

The crowd didn't seem to notice either mistake. They cheered wildly as the song ended. But Star felt like bursting into tears. She didn't need Lola's imaginary psychic to tell her she was on the verge of turning in the worst performance of her life.

The lights were still swirling around, blinking from white to pink to purple and back again. But Star's eyes had adjusted a little by then, as they always did, turning the audience from vague shadowy shapes behind the glare back into people.

She peered out into the crowd, thinking about that scalping story she'd seen earlier that day. Glancing at the first couple of rows, she saw that they were almost completely filled with adults, most of them sitting sedately in their seats while the rest of the audience danced and shrieked around them. Her heart sank. She knew that Mike always reserved a few tickets for important record executives and other VIPs, who weren't always as enthusiastic as her typical fans. But this time she couldn't help wondering if some of the others in the front row were people who just happened to be rich enough to buy the best tickets from scalpers.

It's not right, she thought. *The best tickets should go to the biggest fans.*

Her gaze wandered farther back into the crowd, where most of the people were standing on their seats, bouncing up and down and screaming happily. Quite a few of them were waving T-shirts or handmade signs. Star was used to seeing such signs, which usually said things like WE LUV U STAR! or STAR POWER 4-EVER!

But this time she realized the signs were more numerous than usual, and many appeared to be wordier as well. She squinted past the lights, trying to read some of the closer ones. One girl in about the fourth row was waving a poster-board sign with a photo of Star framed in a heart and a bunch of words she couldn't make out – except for the name JADE written in ugly block letters. Nearby, a pair of preteens were holding either end of a long banner that appeared to be made out of a bedsheet. They were waving it so enthusiastically that Star couldn't read much of it, but she caught the words FAMILY and HOPE.

Star blinked. "Hey," she said into the microphone, her words bouncing out of the speakers and over the crowd. "You there, with the sign." She pointed to the first girl. "Can you bring that up here, please? I'd like to see it. Yours, too," she added, pointing to the pair with the bedsheet.

The fans she'd pointed out looked stunned for a moment. Then, as she smiled and gestured them closer, they squealed and leaped off their seats, pushing their way forward through the crowd.

Star glanced down at the nearest security guards, who looked surprised. "Can you help them out, guys?" she asked with a winning smile. "It's okay – you can bring them right up here onstage."

The rest of the concert goers were murmuring and craning their necks to see what was happening. Star glanced over her shoulder and saw that the band and dancers also looked perplexed. This definitely wasn't part of her usual onstage routine.

Meanwhile the guards were helping the three girls onto the stage. "Thanks, guys," Star said, her every word still echoing through the hall. "Hi there," she greeted the fans with a smile. "Thanks for coming out tonight. I just wanted to get a better look at your signs."

Now, even though all three girls were so nervous and excited that their hands were shaking, Star could clearly see the signs they were holding. The first one, the one with the picture of herself, read JADE MIGHT BE COOL, BUT STAR RULES: WE ♥ YOU STAR! The long banner read GOOD LUCK FINDING YOUR FAMILY, STAR! NEVER LOSE HOPE!

Star put a hand to her heart, so touched that she felt tears spring to her eyes. It was true – her real fans *did* support her! They believed in her, and they cared about her happiness.

"Thank you," she said to the girls, impulsively reaching out and grabbing all three of them into a big group hug. "Thank you so much."

The girls seemed confused and excited and overwhelmed all at once as they hugged her back. The rest of the audience cheered loudly. When Star finally pulled away, the security guards stepped forward to help the three fans back to their seats.

Star grinned out at the audience, suddenly feeling much better about the concert. Who cared about scalpers and the rest of the outside world? As long as she was here, with thousands of her true fans cheering her on, she was going to forget about the rest and do what she loved to do. Maybe she couldn't control the search for her parents, the ridiculous press rivalry with Jade, or even her own stupid dreams. But at least she could give her loyal fans what they came for.

"All right, guys!" she cried, glancing back at the band. "Ready?"

Her band leader nodded. As Star turned back to face the audience and prepared to signal for the next song, she noticed another sign dancing up and down about halfway back in the first section. This one seemed to consist entirely of a very large blown-up photograph, and for a second she thought it had to be the worst picture of herself she'd ever seen.

Then the sign turned slightly, reducing the glare from the stage lights and making it easier to see. Star smiled as she realized it wasn't a picture of her at all – it was one of Dudley. She recognized the photo immediately as one of her favourites from a photo shoot she and her dog had done for a popular music magazine. It showed him sitting up on his hind legs, his moist black lips seeming to smile around the big white plastic bone he was holding in his teeth.

Suddenly Star gasped. That was it!

Ten

Star laughed out loud. She had finally figured out what those scary dreams meant! The crowd cheered. They didn't know why she was laughing, but they didn't seem to care.

"Okay, people!" Star cried into her microphone. "Everybody on your feet – I don't want to be the only one dancing!" She gestured to her band. "Let's go, guys!"

The band launched into the next song. Star snapped into position with her backup dancers, her whole body suddenly brimming with more energy than she'd felt all week.

From: MissTaka

To: singingstar01

Subject: I'M BACK!!!

Hey Star!

Sorry about my stupid e-mail; it's finally fixed now. I got yr phone message; hope yr hanging in! We're fine here, don't worry about us — we're all having a contest 2 see who can make the most reporters curse by not telling

them NEthing interesting about u. Hee hee! Aaron sez he's sure he's winning, but I think yr nans is ahead. She spent about an hour yesterday telling that grey-haired guy from channel 6 how 2 bake the perfect blueberry pie!

NEway, can't wait to hear the inside scoop on Jade — that must have been SOME meeting! Oh, & I already got yr postcard from London. U better remember 2 send me 1 from Italy when u get there! I'm sooo jealous yr going there w/o me!!! (j/k — sorta!) Gotta go, Mom's calling me; more later . . .

Luv ya!

Missy

Star smiled as she read Missy's e-mail the afternoon following the concert. She decided to wait and answer it later — she would have plenty of time to type on the long bus ride to Italy. She saved the message and then clicked off her handheld as Tank eased the tour bus to a stop and hit the button that opened the front doors.

"Here we are," he announced. "Last stop before we head for the English Channel — the Londonia Hotel."

Mike glanced over at Star, who was already clipping Dudley's leash to his collar. "I still don't know why I let you talk me into these things, Star," he said sourly. "Especially when you won't even tell us what it's all about."

"I'll tell you when I come out, I promise," Star said, heading for the door with Dudley at her heels. "I just want to see if I'm right first."

She hadn't told the others about her big brainstorm at the concert the night before. The only one she'd told was Dudley, though she wasn't too sure he'd understood. He was still being a grump, and he had spent most of the long drive down from Scotland whining and scratching at the bus windows.

The hotel had been warned that Star was coming, and security ropes were set up outside, separating her path to the front door from the cluster of waiting reporters. Star had no idea how the reporters had known she was coming to the Londonia. She supposed they must have been following the buses, or maybe someone on the hotel staff had let it slip. In any case, she was relieved to see that the reporters were much fewer in number than before. Just that morning Eddie Urbane had abruptly cancelled part of his current American tour so that he could fly to Milan to attend a big fashion show with his brand-new supermodel girlfriend, and suddenly most of the entertainment world's attention was focused on that.

"Stand aside, coming through," Tank called out as Star hopped off the bus and gave a quick wave to the cameras.

"No questions, please," Mike added gruffly. "We're on a schedule here."

Soon Star was inside the spacious, tastefully decorated lobby of the Londonia. She breathed a sigh of relief, knowing that the hotel's efficient security staff would make sure she wasn't bothered while she was inside.

"Why don't you wait here?" Star told Tank and Mike. "You guys can't follow where I'm going, anyway."

She giggled at the confused looks on their faces and hurried away before they could answer, dragging Dudley behind her. A quick glance over her shoulder confirmed that the men weren't following – they obviously trusted the hotel's security, too.

Soon she was crossing the quiet, shadowy expanse of the empty ballroom. The velvet curtains on the narrow windows had been pulled back, and beams of bright sunlight cut through motes of dust suspended in the still air.

Star headed straight for the ladies' room on the east wall. Pushing open the door, she dragged Dudley inside.

"Come on," she said to the little dog. "Trust me, you'll be happy we came."

She led the way past the sinks and the seating area, heading towards the toilets in the back. Halfway there Dudley's droopy ears suddenly perked up. He let out a wheezy bark and lunged forward excitedly.

Star dropped the leash, allowing him to race on ahead. By the time she reached the closest stall, Dudley had dashed beneath the divider. She swung open the door and looked in. The little pug was on his belly, wriggling under the toilet bowl, his curly tail wagging like crazy.

"Was I right?" Star asked, her voice echoing in the empty, tiled room. "Is it there, Duds?"

She kneeled down on the clean tile floor, peering under the toilet bowl. There was a small crack between the edge of the tile and the smooth porcelain of the toilet – and wedged into that space was a familiar white plastic bone.

"Wow," Star murmured. "I can't believe nobody found this when they were cleaning this bathroom."

But it wasn't really that hard to believe. Unless you were looking for it, it would be easy to miss – the white of the bone blended perfectly with the white of the tile.

Star pried the bone loose with her fingers, and a second later Dudley wriggled backwards, spun around, and pranced proudly out of the stall with the bone clenched firmly in his teeth. Star laughed out loud and clapped her hands as she stood up and followed her dog.

As soon as she'd seen that sign at the concert showing Dudley with his favourite bone, she'd realized that the bone had been nowhere in sight since they'd arrived in Scotland. In fact, she hadn't seen it since finding it in her jacket pocket at the post-awards-show party – just before Manda Smith had entered the ladies room in search of Jade and bumped Star so hard that her jacket had gone flying under the toilets.

Star had realized right away that the bone must still be in the bathroom. No wonder Dudley had been acting so odd – he'd been searching for his favourite toy ever since leaving London! That had to be the explanation for her weird dreams as well. Somewhere in the back of her mind she'd known what was wrong with her dog. That was why she kept dreaming about a white bone and the sound of rushing – or, rather, *flushing* – water. She was subconsciously remembering what had happened. It was just too bad her conscious mind had taken so long to catch on!

She bent down to hug the little dog, who was wriggling all over with happiness. "Feel better now?" she asked. "Sorry about that. I know how important silly little things can be when you're on the road." She smiled and touched her star necklace, relieved that her dream had ended up having such a benign meaning. She felt slightly foolish for jumping to other conclusions; her parents had taught her better than to give up like that. But she wasn't going to worry about it too much. At least it would make a good story to tell Missy now that her e-mail was up and running again!

Soon Star and a much happier Dudley were hurrying towards the hotel lobby. As she rounded a corner in the hall, a girl stepped out of a nearby doorway. Star gasped, recognizing her instantly.

"Jade!" she blurted out. "What are you doing here?"

Jade turned and spotted her. Her pretty face registered shock and dismay before returning to its usual slightly pouty expression.

"I'm staying here, remember?" she said. "What are *you* doing here?"

"Just passing through." Star didn't feel like explaining her errand at the moment. She stared at Jade, her mind suddenly filled with everything that had happened after their last meeting. She took a deep breath. "But as long as we're both here," she said, "I have a question for you. Why did you do it? Why did you say all those mean things about me to the press?"

She was careful to sound curious rather than accusing. For all the trouble Jade's words had caused her over the past few days, she was willing to give the other girl the benefit of the doubt.

Jade merely shrugged, tossing her dark hair over one shoulder. "Hey, I only gave back as good as I got," she said. "You started it, remember?"

"You mean that quote in the *Chat*." Star sighed. "Listen, Jade, I swear I didn't say what that reporter said I did. I never said anything bad about you at all. She twisted my words around and changed them so they sounded totally different from what I actually said. But even so, I'm really sorry if that story hurt you."

Jade looked startled. "Oh," she said. There was a moment of silence. Then she shrugged again. "Whatever. It's just the business, you know?"

Star couldn't help being disappointed by the other girl's response. She'd been hoping for a matching apology – or at least an explanation.

"But why did you tell the whole world about my secret?" she prompted. "I thought I could trust you."

"Hey, I didn't tell the *world*," Jade replied quickly. "Just Stan – my manager, you know." She frowned and glared at Star. "I didn't mean to do it, okay? He was all up on my case about you, like it was *my* fault you got quoted saying that stuff about me in the papers. I just wanted to get him off my back, okay?"

Star gaped at her. "What?" she said. "You mean he blamed *you* for what *I* said? But that's—"

"Forget it," Jade interrupted her brusquely. "Look, I've got to go."

She spun on her heel and disappeared around the corner. Star stared after her. It was a moment or two before she realized that Jade hadn't actually apologized for anything.

Star shrugged. Somehow it didn't seem worth getting upset about.

"Oh, well," she told Dudley. "Come on, let's get back before Mike and Tank come looking for us. They're probably anxious to get back on the road." She grinned as Dudley let out a muffled bark around the bone he was still holding in his teeth. "Yep, I'm excited, too," she told him happily. "Italy, here we come!"

Catch Star's next act

Never Give Up

Star is touring Italy when she gets exciting news: The police have a new lead on her family's disappearance! Star is desperate to fly to Florida where the clues have turned up, but Mike won't let her go because of her commitments, and because he doesn't want her getting in the investigators' way. Star is so angry she sneaks off – in rocker Eddie Urbane's tour jet!

Now Mike is furious with Star, and the media is having a field day. Will star and manager ever forgive each other, or is the tour ruined before it's barely begun?

**Find out in *Never Give Up*,
the next book in the Star Power series!**

star power

by Catherine Hapka

She's beautiful, she's talented, she's famous.

She's a star!

Things would be perfect
if only her family
was around to help
her celebrate. . . .

Follow the
adventures of
fourteen-year-old
pop star
Star Calloway

A new series from Simon & Schuster

She's sharp.

She's smart.

She's confident.

She's unstoppable.

And she's on your trail.